EMILY'S VOICES

A memoir

Emily Knoll

ISBN: 978-1-9998638-4-5;

This paperback edition was first published in 2018

COVER DESIGN BY ANASTASIA SICHKARENKO

Cover image: © Anastasia Sichkarenko 2018

Jacket layout: © Anastasia Sichkarenko 2018

Book layout: John Pullen

Copy-editor: Brenda Stones

Editor: Dennis Hamley

For Fred

With thanks

My thanks for advice, help and encouragement also go to Cherry, Brenda and Dennis

Many of the names and identifying characteristics of people and places have been changed. Emily's experiences are based on real life events.

CONTENTS

Foreword by Dr Susan Shaw

Voice-hearing is a phenomenon which is poorly understood and defined, can cause enormous distress and affects many millions of people. Classically a voice-hearer will hear a voice when no one is around them. Emily's memoir is an evocative, bitter-sweet and moving dialogue of one woman's struggle to understand herself and her voices. For those readers who know little about this area, voices can be experienced as outside or inside one's head, can be someone else's voice or one's own voice. Voices can be heard as a solitary voice or as many, and may be familiar to the person or not. They can criticise, they can state everyday facts or they can be of comfort and encourage. Perhaps surprisingly, they can also be a normal everyday experience for many people when falling asleep or waking up, and one of the common reports is of hearing one's name being called. It has been estimated that up to 15 per cent of the adult population may have heard a voice at some point, sometimes as an isolated event, other times more frequently. The majority of people will not have felt the need to seek help, and indeed probably had no need to do so.

Therein lies the challenge for the psychiatrist, such as myself, in trying to work out the genesis of voices. What is the meaning of them? Does the patient wish to be treated? Having treated many patients for voice-hearing over the years, including Emily, there is no easy answer to these questions. But Emily so clearly shows the terror of hearing voices when she writes of her experiences as an au pair and ultimately her need for treatment. Her voices can come at times of stress, which perhaps gives us a clue to why they start. Voices come from within, even when they are experienced as alien, and I read with interest how Emily's therapist challenged her to accept the voices, to live with them, to live alongside them. I wondered if this has helped her to manage them better, and as part of that process whether eventually they will fade away completely?

Voices are commonly thought of as only occurring in schizophrenia, but are actually a core symptom of many different illnesses. Patients with mood disorders can experience voices that are 'mood congruent', so a voice may make sad and depressing comments if the person is feeling low. The voice can be optimistic and tell the person they are capable of amazing achievements if the person is high in mood. Patients with emotionally unstable personalities or who have suffered trauma may hear the voice of a person who has been cruel or abused them. Emily talks about the different diagnoses she has been given over the years, and this sadly is often the experience of patients whose symptoms can have a kaleidoscopic nature to them, making it difficult to fit them into the rigid diagnostic criteria that psychiatrists use. That is why sometimes for some people it is better to think about treatment and management of voices rather than what a diagnosis might be - after all this may change again and again.

Emily makes the point in her writing that she has taken medication on and off over the years. It can be useful when things are really bad for her, but much of the time she feels she can manage without. This is not the case for some people who need medication continually to control their voices; but for some patients medication as and when they need it can be right for them. Some of my patients over the years have heard voices continually and manage without medication completely. Voice-hearing and treatments are fluid and change according to circumstances, intensity of experience and need of the person.

The support of others is invaluable in the recovery process and can come from many varied and sometimes unexpected sources. Voices can isolate people because of what they say ("That person doesn't like you, stay away from them!") but also because the voice-hearer can worry about how they will be perceived by others if their secret is known about. Support from other voice-hearers, friends, professionals, a partner and family can all help in small ways to prevent the withdrawal of the person from society and help them to believe in themselves. Many of my patients work either in paid or voluntary positions or have returned to study. It is vital for people with mental health problems to do so, as we know that for those patients who are able to achieve this, their prognosis is better. Most people who are employed enjoy the structure, the social contact, the satisfaction of achieving something and the pay. Why is someone who hears voices any different?

Non-psychiatric treatment and support is incredibly important for voice-hearers, so when Emily told me she wanted to apply for a Master's, I was delighted as I knew she could do it. She would acknowledge that at times every day can be a struggle, but she has achieved much through determination and tenacity. I was delighted to be asked to write this Foreword, and hope that Emily's struggle and path to recovery will be an inspiration and source of support to all who read her story.

Dr Susan Shaw, Consultant Psychiatrist, The Warneford Hospital, Oxford, OX3 7JX

Prologue:

The Hospital

I listened to the people talking about me.

"Emily's playing up for attention. Just ignore her," the man with the brittle voice was saying.

Then the woman replied, "I think she enjoys it."

"I think Emily's trying to make us understand," said the person who sounded like a doctor, as he had an authoritative air and always talked about me being ill.

I wanted to be understood, more than they could imagine. But then music started on the rooftop, as if a band was playing. This startled me, as I thought that above me was the rooftop of the psychiatric ward where I was trapped.

I wanted to be invisible, so that these people couldn't pick on me any more. But they didn't seem to want to stop. If only I could be absolutely sure that there were no steps up to the roof above me, but I wasn't. What if the woman and these two men had sneaked up onto the roof to scare me?

I looked up to see a flash of light, as a nurse shone her torch in. It rested on my face, and I turned my head into the pillow. I hated it here. But I was afraid to leave. Listening to the people had been so scary in my flat that the hospital seemed a safer place to be.

I now heard a half-animal, primeval scream of a man beneath me. I shivered in my bed. Wrapping my duvet tighter, I realised that for some patients the hospital certainly did not feel a safer place. I decided that the people who had bullied me at work and in my flat must have followed me to this ward, wanting to torment me. I stared miserably into the dim room, wondering how long it would be before I could go to sleep. I could have asked the nurse for a pill, but maybe I would just fall asleep. The shadows in the room seemed an eerie shape to me. Had the people gone? I held my breath, and listened.

"Emily's waiting for us to disappear," said the woman cruelly.

"We're not going away," the man with the nasal and brittle voice replied.

"Maybe she wants us to go," the doctor said.

I started to play over their words in my head, wondering what they meant by what they had said. *Would they really go? Or was this just another trick to torment me?* I had no idea, and I was stuck here all night. Now that I was in this hospital, there was no escape.

The next morning, I'm in a panic because I need a shower, but I can't get the people to shut up. Every few seconds I need to press a button on the wall to make the hot water start running again, and even then only a small amount drizzles out. I have rubbed some shampoo into my hair, and I need to wait long enough for it to wash out.

"Emily fancies herself," said the woman. "She's such an attention seeker. Now she's putting on weight."

"It's the medication. She has to take it," the man with the brittle voice was saying.

"Better be safe," said the doctor.

I've washed out the shampoo, but I'm still in the shower. It's almost as if I'm frightened to reach for my towel. I don't want my body to be exposed to these cruel eyes watching it, and measuring each curve. It doesn't help that I had anorexia as a teenager, and even now in my twenties I'm still conscious of the way I look.

There's a knock on the door, and a voice says, "Emily, are you in there?"

I realised that it's a nurse doing her checks. "Yes, I'm here," I say, feeling relieved that somebody else is nearby. Can she hear the people as well? A few moments later, I feel annoyed that I'm being checked up on in the shower.

The nurses walk round with their clipboards, writing notes about the patients at different points throughout the day. They seem to spend most of the rest of the time huddled in their office, where I assume they're talking about the patients.

I've been in hospital before for my problems with food, but nothing compares to this time. I wish that the people who keep tormenting me would go away. But whatever I try to do to get rid of them makes no difference. It's as if they want to keep chipping away at me until I erupt. I start to cry, wishing that I had a broom with me to knock at the ceiling to drive the people away.

Three people watching me. There's no space of my own now to retreat to. I reach for the towel and wrap it tightly round me, then I walk through to my small room, and briskly rub myself with my towel. I'm scared to let it slide onto the floor, because the audience above me will see the body that I want to hide.

I take a jumper and a T-shirt from the wardrobe and, keeping the towel round me as if it's a tent, I start to pull on the trousers. Already they feel tighter, and I have only been on this medication for a week. I feel terrified that I will be gaining weight so fast that I will become like the huge women I saw earlier queuing up for more toast. *Which is worse, being fat or having the voices of these people tormenting me? I can't decide.*

I wonder if I should go out to the ward, but earlier a patient grabbed a drink of water and threw it at another patient. I don't want to be in missile range like that. Still, part of me is frightened to stay in here, as these people want to freak me out. I go over to the window and look down on the road. Parked on the right side is the red car that I'm convinced was following me before I came here. If I could go outside, I could read the number plate, but as it is I don't even have my glasses with me to see it. It's here to frighten me; I'm sure of it. My heart's thumping in my chest, and I feel shaky. *Why can't this be a dream, so I can wake up from it? But it isn't one. I'm being stalked like this by the people who keep picking on me, so that I'll kill myself.*

Part 1
Kent

One

When I was a little girl, we lived with my grandparents in a bungalow in a leafy, picturesque village in Kent, because my parents had divorced when I was two years old. This was the 1990s, and my mum escaped for her dinner dances and dates with men in fancy cars, and every morning she drove to work in her red mini. Mostly, our village was where families lived in smart houses, and the men went to work in the city or nearby in one of the towns, and the mums stayed at home with their kids.

I know that my mum felt sad every time she took us to a park on a Sunday and saw mums and dads with their kids, laughing, enjoying a family day out. She filled the space in the best way she knew how. She gave me piano lessons, which I kept asking for, even when Granny got cross that my mum spent so much of her time on me, and not my brother. Mum liked the fact that I was musical, as she was. She also thought that the younger you started a child playing their instrument, the greater the probability they would end up being gifted.

My dad, I didn't know much about. But I was an excellent eavesdropper, and the best time to listen was late on in dinner parties. I remember such an occasion vividly, when I crept downstairs and stood on tiptoe, watching through the keyhole as the chocolates were passed round. I heard them talking about a man called Saul, who people said was my daddy, and I wanted to know more.

"Do the children still see Saul?" asked Sally, my mum's friend.

"No," replied Mum firmly.

"That's very sad," said Sally.

"Emily has stopped asking about him," replied Mum. "I've taken that to be a sign that she doesn't remember him." I saw her top up her glass with sherry.

I must have been four at the time, but those words stayed with me. I realise now that I was curious, even then, as to where I came from. That night a few details were soaked up, and back upstairs, lying in the warmth of my bed again, I cut-and-pasted them into my collage of Daddy. It was a collage where some of the details were missing, so sometimes thinking about my father gave me nightmares. It didn't help that one of my favourite games was looking over at my nightlight, which was shaped like a small cottage with roses growing over the side. I liked to imagine that I could walk inside this cottage and find a lounge with a warm fire, and then one by one I would walk my characters into it. There was Granny, Grandpa, Mummy too, and my little brother Dan, then a space was left on the sofa. Would Daddy come for tea?

I now imagined a knock on the cottage door. Into the room came a tall man with a brown beard like the shepherds that I had learned about in Sunday school. I noticed that he kept looking towards the door, and I felt nervous.

Mum said, "Saul, will you stay for tea?"

I felt anxious until he sat down. He only sat there for a few moments, but it seemed very special.

"Saul!" Mum gasped, as his eyes shifted to the door, making me nervous again. Mum said, "Please stay. The children want to see you."

He stood up, put his cap back on his head, and said, "I need to be going. I've work to be doing."

I didn't say anything. My father walked towards the door. I thought I heard him sigh. I followed him outside the house, but I couldn't keep up with him. My father faded to a dot, then he disappeared.

That made me feel very scared. I didn't like the thought that my father could go away again any time he pleased. Now, when I look back, I realise that I was afraid of feeling that things were outside my control.

My mum and I liked playing Mozart best. I had been stuck on getting the notes right for some time now, and to help there were bright coloured stickers on some of the notes. I played, "Twinkle, twinkle, little star..." Once again I made a mistake, and hearing my mum sigh, I stopped and stared down miserably at the piano.

"Emily, let me play it to you," said Mum.

I can't play it! I said in my head, as I listened to the tinkling sound like bells which my mother made, with no mistakes at all.

"Have another go," said Mum, "this time really concentrating."

So I tried again. But it was no good, as quite soon I played another wrong note.

"No, that's too fast. Play it more slowly," said Mum sharply.

I noticed that the notes I played didn't sound at all like bells, so I stopped.

Just then there was a loud knock on the door. Looking angry, Granny walked into the room and stared at the piano. She spoke to my mum, and said, "Stella, can you stop that piano now. The children need to have their tea and their baths. And the time's getting on."

I was hungry, and was glad to hear that tea would be served up shortly. But also I felt unhappy that my mum wasn't pleased with my piano playing.

Sighing, my mum said, "Mum, I just want five more minutes with Emily, so she can play this piece again."

"Stella, all this piano's ridiculous and it's not fair of you," Granny said. "The children need to have their tea. And Dad and I could do with your help."

I felt awkward being caught up in their cross-fire. Most children get upset when adults have arguments, but I think that I must have been particularly sensitive. It didn't help that my mum argued with her parents so often. I realise now that she found it very uncomfortable living in a house where she had little control over what happened. My mum needed to earn money, as my father paid no child maintenance. This meant that my grandparents provided most of the childcare. So the time she spent with me on the piano was all the more special for her. And I liked to spend time alone with my mum, even if the piano was a big source of tension.

"Well, Mum, we'll stop then," snapped my mum, turning towards Granny. "But in future I want to start Emily's piano lesson earlier. Tonight she couldn't concentrate because she was too tired."

"Stella, it's not fair to blame me," replied Granny. "Maybe you should keep some more nights free in your week to spend with the children. You do go out a lot."

"I need time to myself as well," said my mum, sighing and looking angry.

I seemed to shrink inside then, away from the space of this room with the adults' angry faces. They didn't notice how I felt on the inside. There seemed no way of telling them, and even if I could have said the words, I didn't want to add to the sadness in that room. So I left my mum looking at the music book and followed Granny down the long corridor to the bright kitchen with its heady smell of bread baking, and immediately I felt a guilty relief that I was with her.

One of the highlights of my week was going for a walk with Grandpa and our border collie, Misty, who looked like Lassie from the film. The Bluebell Forest was a favourite walk, and I would watch in awe as Grandpa threw a stick, knowing that it would be returned.

One afternoon, with the bluebells stretching as far as I could see, swaying slightly in the breeze, I got the impression of it being a sea. I felt reluctant to walk in the wood, as the bluebells were so perfect that I didn't want to squash any of them.

"Come on, lass, what are you waiting for?" called Grandpa, in his thick Scottish accent.

How could I tell him that everything felt topsy-turvy? Anyway, Misty was barking loudly and picked up a huge stick in his mouth. Laughing now, I ran into the forest after Misty and Grandpa.

I liked to tell Grandpa stories of what I'd been up to in the week. I always had one collection or another on the go: at that time it was pressing flowers, but I didn't want to pick any bluebells as those were too precious. So I made do with dandelions and snowdrops, for somehow those didn't matter quite as much as bluebells. Anyway, my pictures needed the snowdrops to complete them in the way that I thought they should be in my mind.

I must have been busy telling Grandpa about one of the pictures. "It'll have children in it, and a dog..." But just then I had walked into a nail sticking out from a post, and blood was running down my face. Stunned, at first I didn't even cry.

"Lass, are you all right?" said Grandpa. "Here, have my hankie."

He gave me his best handkerchief, which was white and neatly folded. Dark crimson spots soaked through it, and sobs erupted from my throat. I felt scared.

"That's a bad cut, lass, isn't it?" said Grandpa. "We'd better go to the hospital and get it seen to."

So, still feeling stunned, I climbed into the car and we drove to the local A & E.

I didn't like waiting in the busy place, or the doctor's cold gloved hands touching my face. We then waited longer and I had a bandage strapped onto my head. When my mum arrived from work, I first heard the click click click of her heels.

"How is she?" she asked, urgency in her voice.

I felt more frightened then. I didn't want Mum to be scared too.

"The doctor says she needs some stitches," replied Grandpa. "But she'll be fine. Won't you, lass?"

I nodded.

"Well, I'd better be going," said Grandpa, "or the old lady will be having kittens, worrying what's happened to me."

I knew that he was talking about Granny. Hearing that Granny would be scared too surprised me, and made me start worrying even more.

My mum would later tell me that the hospital was understaffed that day, because there was a strike. So my mum, who had trained as a nurse, helped a doctor to hold me down as the shiny needle went in and out. I was screaming, because there wasn't any local anaesthetic either. But my mum wanted me to have the stitches then and there, to get it over with.

That evening, when we returned to the bungalow, I was rewarded with an eggcup of Smarties. After I'd finished these, the eggcup was filled with more Smarties and I smiled at the treat. I went upstairs to bed, thinking that the pain was a little better too.

Food was something I loved passionately as a child, but it could be a source of envy too. My brother and I were born two years and two days apart, which meant that as young children we had a shared birthday party. For my sixth birthday party, I was given a bright yellow butterfly cake with pink spots on its wings. But I envied the chocolate train cake that Granny had made for my brother, Dan, which had a blue iced face like Thomas the Tank Engine.

"I want that cake," I said, pointing to my brother's.

"But I made you a butterfly, because you asked for one," said Granny.

"I wanted a train," I flatly announced, starting to cry.

"D'you remember that butterfly you drew for me?" asked Granny.

I nodded slowly, sniffing now.

"Well, that's the picture I based the cake on," said Granny. "Here, have a hankie. Let's not have any more tears. Go outside now to blow out your candles."

So I took the tissue she passed me, and went out to the garden where the rest of the family were waiting for me.

"Emily, that's a pretty cake. Aren't you a lucky girl?" said my Aunt Janis in her bossy voice.

I didn't like my aunt, as she sometimes picked on me.

Aunt Janis lit the candles on both cakes. Dan was blowing out his candles. I stared down at my cake, feeling miserable.

"Come on, Emily. Blow out the candles!" said my mum.

But when I only made a half-hearted attempt, she helped me to blow out the rest. She didn't want any scenes in front of her friends and the rest of the family, so she gave me a brisk hug and said, "I'll give you a big slice of the train cake."

"But it's not mine," I replied.

"Well, that's the best I can do," she said.

My mum was a peace-maker: she didn't like arguments, especially when they kept on happening. Now when I look back at that little girl, I realise that when I learned to hold in my emotions it was as if I was not allowed to show my sadness.

There was something else about that day which stands out for me. I remember entering the dining-room and I suddenly stopped, hearing my mum talking to her brother, my Uncle Jack, in a hushed voice.

"I've saved up nearly half the money I need," said Mum. "I need to move out. I want to bring up the kids in my own way. And Mum's so interfering."

"Have you found a house yet?" Uncle Jack asked her. Although my uncle was a sandal-wearing, vegetarian hippie millionaire, he was also a practical man. He must have seen that the dynamic between my mum and my grandparents was very unhealthy.

"I've seen a house I like, that I can just about afford," my mum told him.

Just then I saw my aunt walking into the house, so I went out into the garden.

Later, my mum would describe the act of buying this house as a *fait accompli*. It was an end-of-terrace house in a nearby town, about twenty minutes' drive from where my grandparents lived. We moved out a short time afterwards, with my grandpa shouting at my mum that she was a selfish woman, and Granny sobbing. It would be some six months before we were allowed to see our grandparents again, and in that time I think that I started to develop an internal world that split me off from those around me, in a way that I had designed to give me protection and comfort.

Two

When I was seven, we spent the first Christmas we ever had without my grandparents there. My mum had invited Ruth, the mother of my friend Amy, and Amy and her older sister. Ruth's husband was a pilot, so he sometimes spent Christmas abroad if he was doing a long-haul flight. Mum, who usually stuck to more simple cooking, cooked a roast turkey, with all the trimmings, roast potatoes and other vegetables, and for dessert there was Christmas pudding. By this time I was getting bored, and was thinking about the telly series I'd recently seen of *The Lion, the Witch and the Wardrobe*. I suddenly had an idea.

"D'you know what's behind there?" I said, pointing to a door.

"No, what is it?" asked Amy.

"It's just a door," said Dan.

"Why don't you look?" I suggested to Amy. Amy's curious sparkly blue eyes were fixed on the door. I think I believed at that moment that on opening the door another world would magically appear.

It would be as if Lucy in *The Lion, the Witch and the Wardrobe* had pushed back some fur coats, and behind them she found snow and magical animals like the fawn. The fawn would have some delicious chocolate fudge to give to Amy.

But Amy, who was now peering into the cupboard, came back to the table looking cross. She was about to say something when I saw her mum give her a look, so Amy sat down and took a mince pie that my mum passed to her.

That was when it dawned on me that Amy lived with her parents in a much bigger house than mine. In fact, it even had a swimming pool and a tennis court, and Amy had an enormous bedroom. I now had the thought that maybe they believed I was pretending, as I wished that I lived in a bigger house. My cheeks felt hot, and I stared down at my mince pie. If only I could really escape through that door into a magical world, I thought, where we could have fun.

But one thing that I did like about our house was the fact that from out of my bedroom window I saw a train pass by every half hour. As the weeks passed by, it grew in my mind that my daddy could one afternoon be riding on one of those trains. Looking back, I see a little girl who lost herself in fantasies to escape painful loss, and some of these I borrowed from the books I read. I was an avid reader, and another favourite book was *The Railway Children.* I loved it when the children's father was freed from prison and came back on a train just in time for tea.

Would my daddy be in time for tea? Would he want to hear our news? He'd listen, then he'd be shown the house, the garden and the beautiful magnolia. In the shed where Ben and I had our 'secret den', my daddy would be told how we spied on the neighbours and about the tree house we were building.

So that daddy would know where we lived, I hung from my window a pink pillowcase. It was so bright that he would see it from his train. *I didn't want him to get the wrong house, did I?*

But my mum didn't appreciate this. She came downstairs holding the pink pillowcase, and she had a cross look on her face. "Why was this outside?" she asked me.

"I wanted it there," I said. I didn't give her a fuller explanation, as I thought that would make her angrier.

"Well, you're not to do that again," she said.

"Why, Mummy?"

"Because the neighbours will think we're common."

So I watched her put the pillowslip back into the pile of ironing, and I thought about all the times that my father could now miss our house, because there was no bright pink pillowslip.

He didn't even have our phone number. My mum never saw any of his family either, and it seemed that all my parents' friends had lost contact with him. Into my head came the sad thought that he might never find us.

Though I did not meet my father for over twenty years, I was reunited with my grandparents. On Boxing Day, they came over with big smiles and enormous presents for Ben and me. Mine was tall and oblong, and so large that Grandpa struggled to carry it inside. He set the present down on the dining-room table.

"Well, lass, are you going to open it?" he asked me.

Excitedly I ripped off the paper, and inside was a tall dolls' house. I unlatched the door and looked into its rooms. In the lounge was a tiny grand piano, which even had miniature music propped open upon it. There was a little girl sitting on a chair next to a fireplace, with a ginger stripy cat asleep in his basket.

I suddenly remembered that my mum had said that we could get a kitten. I decided that I'd ask if he could be like this one.

The dolls' house also had a mummy, a daddy, and a little brother living in it, with their two grandparents. But after my grandparents had left, my mum said, "That's a big wind up by your grandmother, putting grandparents in there. We don't live with them any more," she said. She was kneeling beside me in front of my dolls' house, looking at these two little dolls with white hair and smiles on their faces.

"But they're dolls, Mum," I said, walking the granny down the stairs to the kitchen. I sat her down at the table with a miniature cup of tea. "Can I still go and see Granny and Grandpa?" I asked.

Before they had left, Mum had agreed that Dan and I could go round there that afternoon after school.

"Yes, I've said you can," said Mum, looking miserable. And she went out of the room.

Why was she like this? My grandparents had

moved house to be closer to us. When Mum drove us past the cottage where they now lived, it looked very old. It was red brick, with pale green shutters, and some of the windows were wonky. I was looking forward to exploring the inside, and playing on the hill outside.

I didn't like going round to the child-minder's, who Mum had arranged to look after us. She was the mother of a boy in my class. She looked after a toddler and another boy, as well as her two sons and Dan and me. I'd been used to having lots of attention from my grandparents, and not having this any more, as well as having nowhere to escape to that was my own, made me feel miserable.

I really liked writing stories after school, which my Grandpa read and then we'd talk about them. So when I couldn't even have the space to do this, I sat in front of the blaring telly at the child-minder's, stuffing myself with crisps and chocolate bars. One of her kids hogged the remote-control, and decided which channel we were watching. Sometimes I felt so distant from the others' chatter that everything was a blur, and the only sensation I was really conscious of was my stomach bulging against my skirt.

Sometimes, though, I went round to Amy's house after school. If it wasn't raining we'd play tennis outside on the court in their garden. I was competitive at nearly everything, and if I felt certain that Amy was going to win, I seemed to switch off during the game. The fact that she was better at tennis than me made it quite likely that she would win, too.

As her next super-powerful serve sent the ball spinning towards me, I lifted my racket quickly, trying to block it. The ball flew downwards towards the net.

"Sorry," I said.

But Amy was smiling. "I've won! D'you want another game?"

I didn't. Luckily the sky was grey now, and I said, "I think it's going to rain."

"Yeah, it is," said Amy. "Well, let's go inside. I'll show you my sticker collection."

I smiled at her, feeling happier. Amy was shorter than me, skinny with curly brown hair. She was one of the only friends I had at that time, but even then we weren't close friends. I tended to isolate myself, I think because I found it difficult to trust, as I found intimacy to be so challenging. Anyway, that afternoon Amy had linked her arm through mine and together we walked towards her house.

"D'you think it's going to snow?" I asked Amy.

"Don't know. Might do," she said, smiling. "If it does, let's hope we get some days off school. Maybe we can go sledging."

I smiled at her, though I didn't think it likely. *For how would my mum drive me up the hill through the snow to Amy's house?*

The lawn stretched up to Amy's beautiful white house, on the top of a hill. I always felt nervous arriving there, and as we reached the door I was careful to remove my muddy trainers. I walked across the cold tiled floor in just my socks.

"Girls, come and have a warm drink," said Amy's mum. "I got that song, *The Snowman*, earlier. Want to have a listen?"

She handed me a warming hot chocolate with marshmallows floating on the top. I sank into a deep chair as 'We're walking in the air...' started playing.

I now imagined a Snowman tightrope-walking between clouds, and I wanted to be up in the sky with him, too. It was scary, but the singing was so beautiful that I wanted to stay there with him. I so didn't want the singing to stop that when it did, it felt that I had tumbled down into the room with Amy and her mum.

"D'you like it?" Amy's mum asked us.

"It was lovely. One of the nicest songs that I've heard," I said.

She smiled at me, as Amy passed me the chocolate biscuits.

"Let's go and see my stickers," Amy said to me.

"Okay," I said, getting up, feeling almost sorry that I'd be leaving Amy's mum and the music. When I look back at that little girl, I see that this searching for warmth and a sense of connection to families other than my own would contribute to the problems with my identity that I developed later.

Three

When we were still in our first year of living at what I now called the Railway House, Mum got very serious about dating a man called Gary. He drove a flashy blue sports car, and I could tell that he wasn't keen on kids because he virtually ignored Dan and me. But one afternoon we did get the chance to climb into the back of his car, though it meant having to sit on plastic bags.

"I don't want mud on the seat," Gary said to my mum.

I wondered how it could get from our shoes onto the seat, unless we wiped our shoes on the fabric. Still, it was exciting for us being inside a car with a roof that could wind back, and which moved faster than most cars did. My Uncle Jack had a sports car as well, and he was fun and made jokes when we went for a ride in his car, so the fact that this boyfriend of Mum's didn't even speak to us felt strange.

But the roads were very familiar as we drove back into the village where we'd lived with our grandparents. The car came to a stop outside a similar bungalow, and Mum said, "Come on, kids. Get out now, please!"

When we'd got out of the car, Mum said, "Go into the garden and play."

"But it's cold, Mum," I said.

"It won't be for long," she replied.

"Can we play football?" asked Dan.

Gary looked surprised, and said, "I don't want a football breaking my windows."

"But Mum, it's boring if I can't play football," said Dan.

I saw Mum give Gary a look, and then she said to Dan, "Well, be careful. Keep the ball away from the house."

We went through to the garden and played football for some time, but my fingers and feet felt numb and painful. So I decided to go up to the house. To my surprise, I saw that Mum and Gary were sitting at the table eating. In the centre of the table was a roast chicken, and I now was hungry. Thinking that Mum had forgotten to call us, I knocked on the door.

Mum was the one who came to the door, with a worried look on her face. "I won't be long. Just a few more minutes."

"But Mum, I'm hungry!" I insisted.

"Please, Emily. Look, I'll take you both to McDonald's when I've finished."

The prospect of a Happy Meal didn't make the angry feeling inside me go away. I looked across at Dan, who was now standing beside me. I expected him to say something, but he just kicked his football. I felt mad inside then. *Wasn't he as angry as me?*

Realising that I must be the only one of us who thought that this was really unfair of our mum, I did my best to push the feeling down deep inside me.

One school night, a few weeks later, I heard my mum playing Saint-Saëns' 'The Swan' on the cello. I knew instantly that this was the instrument I wanted to learn. Actually, I'd briefly tried a few different instruments, such as the recorder and the flute, but it was the cello's rich tone and the swooping noise it made as my mum's bow crossed the strings that I loved. I asked her to play the piece a couple more times, then I looked through the music alone by myself, and felt happier.

Cello lessons started shortly afterwards, on a three-quarter size cello which my mum had bought for me. My teacher, Mary, was tall, slim and beautiful, with long, dark hair. She was a retired singer and cellist, and taught her pupils in an impressive music-room with vast windows looking over the lawn. Often her husband would be mowing the grass outside during my lessons, making immaculate stripes of lighter and darker green.

Unlike the piano, I took to the cello without a fight, really enjoying learning all the notes and their fingerings. Quite quickly I progressed to short simple pieces, but the biggest triumph of these lessons was the fact that it wasn't my mum who was in charge. I liked having a teacher who encouraged me to play for myself, in an expressive way.

"You could bring out those lower notes more, like this," said Mary, during one afternoon lesson after school.

She picked up her own cello from its stand, and played the bars from the piece again. I loved the deep sounds best, so after listening carefully I pressed my bow more into the string and pulled it across gently. But just as I was really beginning to enjoy the sound, the doorbell rang.

Mary got up to answer it, saying, "That'll be your mum. Why don't you play the piece from start to finish?"

This suggestion made my heart sink, as my mum had a habit of always picking up on something wrong that I'd played.

But this time she came in with a worried look on her face.

"We thought we'd give you a little concert," said Mary.

But my mum was looking at her watch. "Sorry, it's just that I don't want to get stuck in the traffic. I'm going out this evening."

I felt disappointed and started to put my cello away. Nowadays, my mum seemed to prefer going out with Gary to helping me with my music. The fact was that she seemed interested only when it suited her.

But then, one weekend night, I found my mum sobbing on the kitchen steps. I felt so scared that I was going to creep upstairs to bed again. But just then our ginger kitten, Tigger, came in the door, and my mum turned round. As I bent to stroke Tigger I saw that tears were streaming down Mum's cheeks. Then I saw that she was holding a glass of wine.

"Mum, what's the matter?" I asked her.

"You wouldn't understand," she said, taking another long sip of her wine.

"What, Mum?"

"It's Gary. He's dumped me, the two-timing bastard."

For a few moments I felt happy, thinking that I'd have more of my mum's attention again, and that I wouldn't have to see that horrible boyfriend any more.

"But Mum, you've got us kids," I said to her.

"I know, darling," she said, giving me a tense smile, and then a close hug.

I went upstairs to my bedroom, but I didn't get into bed straightaway. Going through my head was the fear that things kept changing, and seeing my mum upset like that made me realise that her world was shaky too. For some time now I'd tried to keep my worries further away from me by repeating little sayings that I'd invented. They were quite similar to prayers, only these asked for very specific things. "*Please keep Granny and Grandpa safe, and Mummy too, and Dan and me. Don't let us get sick with the chickenpox or deadly germs.*" Looking back, it was similar to how, a couple of years earlier, I'd walked my whole family inside the warm, snug cottage that was my nightlight. It was as if by acting out these fantasies, I felt that I could make them come true, giving me a place where I felt safe and loved.

Around this same time, I was starting to establish rituals and ways of thinking that gave me a greater sense of control. But my world was about to alter dramatically. My mum had felt very alone after Gary dumped her, so she soon started dating again.

This time it was Justin, who was taller with grey hair, even though he was just a few years older than my mum. If my mum was in earshot, he would chat to Dan and me about what kind of a day we'd had; but when she wasn't near, he'd ignore us.

One afternoon, he was driving us all home from swimming, and he ignored us in the car as well.

"D'you not like swimming?" I asked Justin.

He didn't reply, which made me feel cross. "Justin, I asked you something. Why don't you answer?" I muttered.

"Emily, don't be rude!" my mum snapped, as if this was my fault.

"I don't like swimming when there are lots of noisy children around, that's for sure," he replied. "I thought I was going to be spending today just with your mother."

"You didn't have to come swimming with us," I muttered.

"Emily!" shouted my mum. "Sorry, Justin, I don't know what's got into her."

I turned to Dan for back-up, but he was plugged into his computer game, and was ignoring everyone.

I realise that I must have felt very alone that day. As the elder child, I probably noticed more the change in our family dynamic, as this man wanted more and more of my mum's attention. As money was tight, with my father paying no child maintenance, my mum would often teach the piano through the evening after working all day at the office. Some nights she even brought home extra typing from her office. This left little time for Dan and me, but when my mum started dating this man, we found ourselves spending increasing amounts of time at our grandparents' cottage, including having our evening meal there. It made me feel confused that my mum suddenly switched gear like this.

My primary school had started to notice my rituals, which over time were taking up increasing amounts of my attention, so that I found it difficult to engage with others. Mornings often began with guided writing, and I became preoccupied with making my writing so neat that the letters filled exactly half the space between the lines and joined together smoothly. Whenever I made a mistake, I crossed out the word and started a new page.

My teacher grew concerned by this behaviour, and one morning she said, "Emily, your writing's very neat as it is. You don't need to start a new page."

"I wanted to start again," I said. I thought that if the writing looked neat enough, then I'd have good luck for the rest of the day. For I now equated neat handwriting with things going right for me.

"But if you carried on, you might finish the exercise," said my teacher.

I didn't reply. I now had the scary thought that something really upsetting might happen to me or someone I cared about if I didn't write out the passage again, more neatly.

And so this obsessive pattern of thinking eventually encompassed not only nearly everything I did, but also what I said. I couldn't say a line to someone without replaying it in my head. Being so careful over what I said made it even harder than it had been before to form friendships with other children. I felt so fragile and nervous that I preferred to withdraw. It didn't help that around this time my one friend Amy had moved to a new house and a different school, so I found myself more alone.

Sometimes now I'd avoid others at break-time by squeezing under a railing behind the classroom block and retreating to a gap in the hedge; this spot let through just enough light to read by, so I'd read a favourite book and eat a chocolate bar.

One break-time when I was reading, I was interrupted by the loud voice of Kevin, a boy in my class who bullied whoever looked to be an easy target. "Hey fatso, what you doing?" he yelled.

"Nothing," I shouted back, hastily pushing the book away, so that he wouldn't see it. "Go away. I'm not talking to you."

"Leave her alone," another boy said. I then saw the face of Matthew, a kinder boy, looking at me too.

They did go away, and for a few moments I felt relieved. But then there was this painful loneliness, as if I was in a bubble by myself.

My teacher picked up on my difficulties, and called in outside professional help. One afternoon as I went to meet my granny at the gate, there was a lady standing beside her with a smiley face.

"Mrs Thorpe is coming home with us for tea," said Granny.

"Hello, Emily," said the lady. "It's nice to meet you. I'm wondering if I can have a chat with you? Your granny tells me that you've got a dolls' house. Maybe you can show it to me?"

When we got back to the cottage, I relaxed more and was pleased that the lady showed interest in my dolls.

"These are lovely," she said, holding up the little girl doll. "Did you enjoy making these?"

"Yes, I made that one," I said. I was exaggerating,

as Granny had made the dolls from pipe-cleaners and cotton wool stuffed into fabric. She used a foam ball for their heads, and I'd just painted the faces.

Perhaps the lady had picked up on the fact that I was withdrawn from other children at school, as she now said, "What other interests do you have?"

"I play the cello. I've just joined an orchestra. We're learning 'Peter and the Wolf' this term," I replied.

"That sounds fun," she said. "And have you made some friends at orchestra?"

"Yes, with Sarah," I said. "I sit next to her. She plays the cello too."

I wondered afterwards whether calling Sarah a friend was an exaggeration. In the orchestra break we had our drink and biscuits together, sometimes taking them outside with the others. But I usually listened as she and the others talked, finding it difficult to chat with them. I didn't want to say the wrong thing, and have to replay it in my head during the second half of the rehearsal, as this would interfere with the music we were playing.

After the lady had finished asking me questions, she went to talk with my grandparents. Curious as to what they might say, I followed behind them and listened in to the conversation taking place in the kitchen.

"I'm upset that someone's jumped to the conclusion that she's unhappy here with us," said Granny, sounding cross. "We do our best for her, don't we, Alan?" she said to my grandpa.

"Vera's always running them to places, and cooking meals for them," Grandpa said.

"And Alan helps Emily and her brother with their

homework," said Granny.

"Yes, I can see that Emily is well cared for. And I also see that she's happy," replied the lady.

"So she'll still be coming to us after school?" said Granny.

This question made me worried, so I pushed open the door. "I can still come here, can't I?" I said quickly. "I don't want to go back to the child-minder's again."

"Yes, don't worry, I don't see why not," the lady said, giving me another of her bright smiles.

But inside I didn't feel entirely reassured. For if a stranger could make the decision about whether I still came here, she could equally decide to stop this. And change would be my greatest fear.

Four

When I was nine, my mum made the decision to marry Justin. They agreed first of all that we should move to a large house where the four of us could live together. But this plan was interrupted when my mum became dangerously ill after a routine sterilisation went disastrously wrong. Her bowel was perforated, requiring an emergency operation. The first time I saw my mum in the hospital was a great shock: she was attached to several drips, and her face was deathly pale.

"How are you both?" she asked Dan and me.

"Okay. How are you, Mum?" was all I could say, still stunned.

"I've missed you both –" said Mum, breaking off with a look of agony on her face.

"Stella, shall I get the nurse?" asked Granny.

Mum nodded, and Dan and I were bustled out. Dan looked as frightened as I felt.

My mum was kept in hospital for several weeks, and during this time my obsessive rituals became more focused around the paranoid fear of being killed by germs. But my most frightening ritual focused on being touched: I didn't want anyone to touch me, however inadvertently, if I was having an 'unlucky' thought at that moment. This meant a thought that was negative about either someone I cared about, or about something that might happen in the future. Being so vigilant to these rituals was very challenging and tiring.

One afternoon, just as I was thinking *I don't want to visit Mum in hospital,* Dan knocked into me as he was kicking his football out into the garden.

I couldn't stop worrying about this, as I now had the scary thought that Mum could get sicker, because of this unlucky 'coincidence'. My granny could not manage to console me, and explained my difficulty to Aunt Janis.

But my aunt did not have the same patience and said, "For goodness sake, Emily, that's ridiculous. Just start acting normally."

Feeling upset, my lip quivered as I did my best not to cry.

"She thinks that something bad will happen to her mum as she didn't want to visit her earlier, isn't that right, Emily?" said Granny, looking over at me.

I nodded. "Well - yes," I said, wanting reassurance from someone that Mum would be okay.

Aunt Janis gave me a brisk smile, and said, "Well, nothing bad is going to happen. And your mum's getting better, so she'll be home soon."

I did my best to smile, but what she said did not make me feel better, as quite soon my mum would be marrying Justin, and already plans for their wedding were being discussed.

I remember vividly the day I was measured for the bridesmaid's dress. The material was cream with miniature gold bows on it, and there was to be a lacy collar and a gold ribbon sash. I had seen the pattern for the dress lying on my granny's table, but I didn't like it. In fact, I wouldn't have liked any bridesmaid's dress, as I didn't want the wedding to take place.

"Emily, stay still, or this hem will be uneven," snapped my mum.

"Ow!" I yelled, as a pin stabbed my ankle.

"I told you to stay still," muttered my mum.

"I don't even want to wear a dress," I said.

"Well, you can't go up the aisle in a pair of trousers," said Granny, who then smiled at me.

But I didn't want her to lighten the atmosphere. I shouted, "Mum, I don't see why I have to be a bridesmaid. I don't want you to marry Justin."

"Enough!" shouted my mum. "Emily, it's not your decision who I marry." She looked upset as she said this.

What I didn't tell my mum was that for weeks now I had been playing fantasies through my head of the possible obstacles that could stop the wedding from taking place. I imagined Justin deciding that he didn't want to marry a woman who had two kids. Justin also had two young sons from his first marriage, and he didn't see them any longer. What if Mum discovered that this was because they hated him? Or maybe my mum would find someone kinder and more fun to marry?

Right up to the moment of the wedding, I imagined something would happen to stop Justin arriving at the church. So it was a great shock when the 'Wedding Anthem' really blasted from the organ. I felt like crying, but I didn't want to ruin things for my mum. So I watched my steps carefully so that I wouldn't trip as I went up the aisle, as we all sang the hymn. But all the time I felt detached from myself, as if I wasn't really there. Looking back, I think it must have been a defence mechanism to 'split myself off' like that, so that I wouldn't have to inhabit a reality I didn't want.

At the reception afterwards, a fantastic feast had been prepared by my granny, with dishes set out on a long table in my grandparents' garden. I helped myself to a second slice of chocolate gateau and heaped on the strawberries.

"That's a very pretty dress you're wearing," said my mum's friend, Sally.

I tried to manage a tiny smile, but it was no use. Tears slipped down my cheeks, and Sally said kindly, "It's a big day for all of you, isn't it?

I knew that what she meant by this was *a big change.*

Nervously, I twisted the gold locket that my new stepdad had given me earlier at the reception. I actually quite liked the present, only I wished that he hadn't been the person to give it to me.

Not long after that, all the guests trooped out to see my mum and stepdad drive off, their car decked out with pale pink ribbons and balloons.

My mum came and found me. "Emily, give me a kiss before I go."

Knowing that she was leaving for a weekend in Paris with Justin, I yelled, "No, I don't want you to go!"

"Please, let's not have a scene," she said. "This is

my wedding day."

So I let her kiss my cheek, and then everyone else was saying goodbye and I lost my mum to a cloud of confetti.

In my new bedroom, there was a large cupboard full of clothes. But sometimes, when I was practising my cello, I'd imagine that I was inside on a stage, playing to a large audience who were spellbound by my music. Each note carried them to the next, and nobody wanted me to stop. I felt I needed to become famous. I had recently watched a film with my mum about the famous cellist, Jacqueline du Pré. So I acted out playing with Jacqueline's intense movements, my whole body swaying with the cello. It was as though there was no space in the music where I could play as me.

Once they were back from honeymoon, my cello practice used to make Justin furious. My mum started asking me not to practise when he was in the house. I'd make angry comments to Mum about this when he wasn't around. Sometimes I'd hear Mum and Justin arguing downstairs. Justin's bad temper seemed to be increasing, and I felt too scared to be rude to Justin's face. But why couldn't Mum, Ben and I go back to the Railway House to live, just the three of us?

And so, increasingly unhappy, I decided to spend more time outside the house. Luckily, I'd met two girls who lived round the corner to hang out with. Rebecca was the same age as me, and very attractive with curly auburn hair, green eyes and a stunning figure. Already she was interested in make-up and trendy clothes. But her younger sister, Kelly, was tomboyish with short brown hair, and she was always plotting fun things for us to do.

The trouble came when the nights drew in, and I was going round to their house most evenings. Justin had told Mum that he didn't want Dan or me inviting friends back when he was at home. My mum didn't seem to think there was anything wrong with this. If Kelly or Rebecca, or their parents, thought it was strange or rude that they never got invited over, they never said anything about it. But I felt very awkward. Did they think that I didn't want them round? Had they worked out that my stepdad was unsociable?

One school evening, I was upstairs with the sisters in Rebecca's bedroom. Rebecca was painting my nails a plum purple colour. I thought they looked really stylish. Inside I was feeling quite sad, as I was getting bullied at school for being chubby, and I really wanted to fit in more. And so something made me pluck up the courage to say to Rebecca, "D'you think I could do with losing some weight?"

Rebecca suddenly looked awkward, and said, "Well, maybe a few kilos."

"I wouldn't worry about it," said Kelly in a bold voice. "Has someone said you should lose weight?"

"No, I just thought I'd look better," I said. But in fact, my mum had started telling me that I should cut back on the chocolate and crisps that I consumed.

Rebecca was now painting my other hand carefully. "I worry about my weight," she said.

"But you're skinny," I replied. I felt envious of her slim frame and gentle curves. I now remembered that her mum encouraged her to eat more chocolate. I wished that I could have Rebecca's sense of control when it came to eating. This thought about my shape didn't dwindle away, because my preoccupation with food and eating was to grow over the following months. And I was on my way to developing another obsession.

Five

A year later, when I was about thirteen, my weight had dropped to six and a half stone. Looking back now, the level of obsession is surprising and frightening. I was under pressure from my family to achieve both academically and with my music, and perhaps my low self-esteem made it easier for me to focus on controlling what I ate. I gradually cut out foods that I thought were fattening, until eventually I was restricting what I ate to just melon and low-fat yoghurt. I was very secretive and regularly hid food during meals. I also wore baggy jumpers and jeans to conceal my weight loss. When the problem was spotted by Granny and an appointment made with the GP, anorexia had taken such a grip that I lied to the doctor, as I didn't want his help. Before long my periods stopped, and white downy hair started to grow on my arms and tummy. I stopped wanting to see my friends and the boyfriend I had met at a youth club, as they would encourage me to eat. Then, there was a family holiday with my mum and stepdad in Spain, where there were terrible rows at mealtimes.

When I arrived back in England I was promptly admitted to a clinic that specialises in teenage anorexia. There I had no option but to eat the three meals a day that were put in front of me, strictly counted by calories. Otherwise I knew that I would be force-fed high-calorie creamy liquid food through a tube. While I did make friends with some of the other girls at the clinic, I also learned their tricks, such as secretly bingeing on cereal and water before I was weighed by the doctor. Eventually, after three months, I reached their target weight and was discharged. I knew that if I lost weight again I would be readmitted. The doctor had encouraged me to be more independent and to go back to my mum's after school. So I used to eat with my mum and stepdad in the evenings in front of the telly.

I vividly remember one night a few weeks after I had gone home. My mum had just handed me my dinner, which was a vegetarian lasagne, saying, "Be careful, it's hot."

I had pushed some lasagne onto the fork, and was blowing at it to cool it down. The telly was on, but I don't remember what I was watching. I could never concentrate on anything much when I was eating.

That was when I heard the words, "You have to eat it. You know that."

It was a loud woman's voice. I realised that it sounded like the doctor, Helen, from the clinic.

I looked over at my stepdad, but he was drinking his wine as if nobody had spoken.

I looked behind me. The door to the hallway was open. *The doctor couldn't be there, could she?* I put down my tray, and went out to the hall. The hall was empty, and walking down to the kitchen, I found my mum getting a dish out of the oven.

"Are you eating your dinner?" Mum asked me.

"Yes, Mum," I muttered.

My mum's voice didn't sound similar to Helen's deeper, posher voice. The clinic was miles away in London. I felt shaken as I went back down the hall to the lounge. There was nothing to explain the voice, which was as real as if the doctor had been speaking to me. I was afraid that I would hear the voice again. I sat on the sofa, listening for her voice. But I only heard the noise of the telly. After a few moments, I picked up my fork and started eating the creamy lasagne.

I remember putting the voice out of my mind then. While I don't remember forming any explanation for hearing the doctor's voice at that time, in retrospect I think that Helen's control over my life in the clinic could explain this. Also, her control over me continued while I lived at home, for I knew that I wasn't allowed to lose any weight. I was also going through a stressful time. It was very difficult for me to readjust to being at home and returning to my school, where I felt unhappy and isolated.

Years later I know that there is no logical explanation for why I heard this voice, which sounded like the doctor speaking to me. After hearing the voice I didn't return to this event in my mind. It was as if I had dissociated the distressing experience. It had just not happened. This was my way of coping with it.

For the next fourteen years, I did not hear voices. I did have some turmoil in my life, though. When I was fourteen I spent a period of five months in foster-care, because I developed bulimia which triggered terrible rows at home with my mum and stepdad. Sometimes Justin had difficulty in controlling his anger, and my bulimia made him explode. My teachers at school had noticed finger-mark bruises on my arms from when my stepdad had pulled me away from the fridge, or dragged me down the stairs after I had stolen food.

It was a relief to escape the arguments and tension at home. In foster-care I sometimes played truant from school, and in the foster-parents' home I found it impossible to study with the loud telly playing in the background. My bulimia also escalated out of control with me stealing food, and on occasions I let the other boy in foster-care take the blame. I began to abuse laxatives, taking handfuls of them as a way of trying to control my weight.

One afternoon at school I became very frightened as I passed blood in my stools. Fearing the worst, I decided to get help from my grandparents, whom I hadn't seen since I had gone into care. I went to their house, and there was Grandpa sitting in his garden as Granny was out at the shops. He offered me a glass of orange squash and told me to wait for Granny. Granny soon arrived, and I blurted out the whole story to both of them: how unhappy I was in foster-care, and how scared I was of the blood that I'd passed in my stools that day.

Granny told me that she was 'very cross' with my mum, and I was very welcome to live them if that was what I wanted. It turned out that Social Services had never contacted my grandparents when the decision was taken to put me into care.

My grandparents were kind and supportive to me over the months that followed. But there were rows, as Granny locked away the food in an effort to make me break the binge-cycle of repeated vomiting and laxative abuse.

I really resented her control at times, and on one occasion I grabbed at some very expensive china cups and saucers. They had belonged to Granny's grandmother, and were proudly arranged on a shelf, but in my rage I smashed them on the hard floor. Granny was kind enough to say afterwards that 'people are more important than things'.

I was able to concentrate on my studies again, and I went on to win a music scholarship to a local boarding school. Then in the summer I took my GCSEs, and gained excellent grades.

At boarding school I made friends, and a couple of these female friends remain close friends today. I went on to study History at York University, with one of these friends called Beth. I enjoyed my new-found independence, and regularly went clubbing and to parties. I had two serious relationships with boys at university, while also squeezing in a lot of studying. I loved learning about the Romans.

Undoubtedly the saddest event during these years was losing my grandpa when I was aged twenty. He died slowly, from a series of strokes that gradually robbed him of his capabilities and dignity. At the end, he'd become a shell of a man, connected to various tubes in the dreary ward of a hospital. When I saw him for the last time he didn't speak at all, and only lifted his hand after being prompted by Granny.

I wanted to cry, but Granny was giving me one of her tight-lipped smiles, so I held back.

After Grandpa had passed away, I remember wishing that I could hear his voice. I never did. I felt a tremendous sense of loss, as Grandpa had understood me. Looking back I realise that Grandpa had been in many ways a substitute father figure.

Although I was still free of distressing voices in these years, I often felt fragile inside. I kept returning to my earlier fear of losing my equilibrium. I remembered the snowman in the song I had loved as a child, 'tightrope-walking between clouds': that feeling of wanting to be in the sky with him, but frightened all the time of falling. This was how it felt to be me.

This sense of dread persisted even when I played the piano. One time as a teenager I remember performing at a recital. My palms felt sweaty, and I kept worrying that my hands might slip from the keys. My first piece was Debussy's 'Dr Gradus ad Parnassum', which moves fast and involves crossing hands. I counted in my head the beat that I wanted, but when I started I was playing the notes even faster. I had to concentrate on stopping my fingers tripping up over each other.

The difficulty was that I felt increasingly conscious of the audience who were listening. As my fingers sped up and down the keys, I began to obsess about making a mistake. They'll hear any mistake, I told myself. My concern about playing perfectly now stopped me from enjoying the notes. Then I heard the A flat - a wrong note - and I winced inside. I carried on, but then there was another jarring mistake. In the end my fingers ran away completely.

I had to stop.

In my life itself, I often worried about making mistakes, and what people's reactions might be. I feared rejection most of all, and I would often hide my true feelings. For example, when my brother Dan had little to do with me after my anorexia, I didn't tell him that this made me upset and angry.

I still found solace in my own company, and while I had friends during these years, I also spent long periods of time on my own. Even when I had a boyfriend, I found it hard to trust and be emotionally intimate. I think this is why my relationships often finished after a year or two, as any boyfriend felt I was holding back something of myself.

Part 2
London

Six

It might have been in the middle of January when I looked up from my bedroom desk and heard voices coming from the other side of the wall. I was working as an au pair, and staying in my employers' flat, so I thought they might be the couple I was working for. But it was after nine in the evening, when Nigel, my employer, usually cooked dinner for his wife, Gloria, in the kitchen down the corridor.

I turned down the Bach I was listening to and concentrated on the voices. "She's spending a lot of time alone," a male voice said.

"She's probably paranoid," said a woman's voice in a spiteful tone.

I felt numb. *Why did they think that? Were the couple spying on me?*

They were chattering again. My heart thumped against my ribs as I struggled to follow their words.

"She's not doing the job properly," the woman's voice was saying.

"She can't cook," the man replied. "She burned

the kids' salmon tonight."

"And she doesn't clean up properly," the woman's voice, nasal and bitter, replied.

Her tone was very critical. It was the sort of thing that my granny might have said.

Then I stared abruptly at the wall. *These were the couple outside, surely?*

A memory flooded my mind of the voice I'd heard briefly in the flat where I had lived a few months earlier in Canterbury. This man's voice was perhaps warmer than the voice that I was hearing now. But then, when I had searched for this voice in the garbage-shed behind the wall, I had found no one. Sometimes that earlier voice teased me, seeming to come from the other side of the wall. I had even pulled out the rubbish and overcome my fear of spiders by crouching down to enter the doorway. I shone my torch around, but didn't see anyone. With nothing to explain it, I had put it down to being a sort of half-phantom. I couldn't say that it was entirely disembodied. Somehow it seemed that a person was really there.

A few months earlier I had left a teacher's training course, because I hated it. It was Granny's idea that I become a schoolteacher, not mine. After leaving the course, I then worked in a referral unit for disadvantaged teenagers in Canterbury for four months, before I quit this job as well to have the time to write a novel. It was when I was very isolated that I had begun to hear the voice.

These voices seemed to project through the wall in my employers' flat. Now, the people spoke indistinct chatter, and I strained to listen. I wondered if it would make a difference if I were in a different flat, miles from here.

"She's schizophrenic. That's what I think," said the spiteful female voice suddenly.

A chilling sensation spread through me, as I heard this terrifying label, and started to wonder again if this really was the couple talking about me. I had been in this job for two months, and never before had I heard them talk in a nasty way about me.

I got up and moved across to the window to stare out at the shadow of the wall. I listened again to the voices. They were quieter now, like murmurs. This made me afraid again. If these were real people, they would be quieter on this side of the room. I wished I had a friend here who could go into the next room to check if the couple were discussing me. Better still, I wished I could be round at a friend's now.

But I was here. For a moment, I thought about calling a friend. I hadn't told my friends about the voice I used to hear. What if these were the same kind of voices? They would think I was crazy.

I wanted to shout out, *Just go away!* But fear of the couple's reaction stopped me. All the same, I couldn't bear having this couple who I didn't know well spying on me and judging me...

Could I?

Taking the au pair job was one of the worst decisions that I ever made. I had only been the English tutor for the couple's two sons for a couple of months, when at the start of one lesson their father, Nigel, had offered me the au pair job, which would mean living in as well as tutoring the boys, who were aged ten and twelve. I remember that Nigel's wife, Gloria, had looked surprised, even upset, and she had said to me, "You're too qualified for this, I don't think you'll want the job."

At the time I was working as a ward clerk in the dementia unit in a busy hospital during the day. I liked the old people, but it was sad and depressing seeing their loss of dignity and bewilderment, and in particular one old man's angry outbursts. I would travel in the afternoons to do the tutoring, and then go home at night, exhausted and tense. Spending more time with the couple's sons sounded like fun, as I had enjoyed tutoring them. They seemed a happy family, affectionate and considerate of each other. I thought their job offer was generous, as the couple made it clear that I would get four or five hours free during the day to do my own thing, so I told them how much I appreciated the offer of a more committed job.

The advantages of the post were that I lived closer to my friends, while the free daytimes gave me the chance to work on my creative writing. But I struggled so much with my anxiety around the job that I usually went to a nearby café to drink a cappuccino and attempt to read a book. I just didn't have the focus to write my novel.

My eating disorder had meant that I had resisted Granny's efforts to teach me how to cook when I was a teenager. This was made more difficult by the fact that food had been locked away inside my grandparents' pantry, so that I couldn't binge on it. So now, staying with a family where I was expected to cook kids' food each evening made me feel very anxious; I kept getting the timings wrong, burning the meat pies or even the asparagus.

For many years the family had employed au pairs who had also lived with them. The previous au pair had been younger than me - in her late teens - and she hadn't had difficulty with this job; she knew how to cook shepherd's pie from scratch. The couple at least tried to keep me with them by giving me simpler dishes to cook than those which the previous au pair had made. But even these I couldn't get right. I was now angry that Granny had encouraged me to take this job, when I had been ambivalent about doing so.

The family I lived with was very wealthy. On the second day after I moved in, Nigel, my employer, had pulled a tin of salmon out from the cupboard saying, "This red salmon is for special occasions." He'd paused for a moment. "One tin costs five pounds." His piercing blue eyes bored into mine, making his point.

"Yes, I'll be careful to use the other tins of salmon," I responded dutifully, anxious to please him. His shrewd look relaxed, knowing he'd won the exchange.

The morning after I'd heard the voices in my bedroom, I was doing chores in the kitchen. I had stacked the dishwasher, and was sorting the family's socks into piles. I'd felt disturbed by hearing the voices the night before. I stared at the beige wall, waiting for the new voices to start again. I wondered if there'd be two voices, which meant they could talk about me. I didn't like that.

"She wants to be understood. That's what I think," said a neutral man's voice suddenly.

I now felt frightened. This neutral man's voice

sounded older and wiser than the brittle, clipped voice from yesterday. I didn't like the idea of someone explaining me.

I went out into the corridor, but the only sound was the maid vacuuming the children's playroom. Nigel now appeared and said, "Can you collect some dry cleaning for me?"

"Yes," I shot back. "Is there anything else?"

"No, that's all," he replied, smiling warmly.

I didn't expect him to look so pleased. I had thought that he and Gloria were being nasty about me last night, when I had heard what sounded like their voices outside my bedroom. Feeling confused, I went to fetch my coat and bag from my bedroom, as I was going to meet my friend Daniel for lunch. Daniel was a librarian, who worked at a nearby university.

I felt scared now that the new voices would start when I was with him. I was very attracted to Daniel. He was eight years older than me, a highly intelligent, kind man, and single. Daniel was also "a friend with benefits", in the sense that from time to time I'd have casual sex with him. It was often highly pleasurable sex, and the fact that it didn't involve commitment made me feel happier, because I feared emotional intimacy and the risk of rejection.

I didn't want to tell Daniel about the voices. He might think I was crazy, and I was scared I'd lose him as a friend. I had met Daniel just a year after Grandpa's death at a housemate's party, and he was the man whom I had trusted most since then.

Outside it was raining, and I had to wait for a few minutes at the iron gates before Daniel arrived. Cars were passing, and as they rushed past me I thought about my fear that the voices might start again. So I was relieved when Daniel arrived. There he was, tall and slim, with dark, wavy hair, and warm brown eyes.

"Hello. How's things?" he asked me.

"Mixed. I hate the job," I said.

"Oh, I'm sorry to hear that," he replied. "Shall we go and get some lunch in the park?"

I now remembered that Daniel had told me that Gloria had phoned him shortly after I'd started this job, and he'd provided a reference for me. What had happened early on was that I had burst into tears when I was confronted with cleaning the mud off the family's shoes after a short walk in the country. My obsessive-compulsive disorder had become transparent, because I couldn't cope with so much dirt, so Gloria had clearly been concerned about me working for them. Daniel had told Gloria that he thought that 'the job would be good for Emily'. Now I worried that I'd disappoint him, and it wasn't that long since my failure at doing the teacher's training course.

The rain had come on more heavily, so we found a covered seating area in the park beside the food stall. Daniel bought us sandwiches and cappuccinos. I was quiet: I really wanted to tell him about the voices, but I couldn't.

"So what's wrong with the job?" he asked me.

"I'm rubbish at the cooking," I said. "I thought that I was going to be mostly tutoring their kids, not being a skivvy. Gloria's giving me more and more chores to do, like the family washing. I'm not getting time to work on my novel."

"Well, if it's this bad, why don't you leave?"

Daniel suggested, and he took a long sip of his cappuccino. He was looking at me, as if he expected a reply.

"I can't. I haven't got any money," I said.

"Well, you could stay in the YMCA near here. It's twenty quid a night," he replied. "I would offer for you to stay at my place, but I'm having building work done at the moment."

His tone was kind, but his comment struck me as detached, as if he didn't get my situation. I had moved lots of books and clothes into the room in the couple's flat, along with my orthopaedic chair and cello. *Where would all my things have to go?*

"She wants him to help. No boyfriend, I expect," the man's voice, nasal and brittle, said suddenly.

"She's on her own," a neutral male voice said.

I looked over my shoulder. *These men were behind the bushes, surely?*

"You're very quiet," Daniel said. "Are you all right?"

"Yes. It's just that I'm very unhappy there," I replied.

"Well, I don't know what else to suggest, other than you move out of there."

The voices were chattering again.

"The woman's being a real bitch to me," I said, the woman being Gloria.

"Well, she's old enough to be your mother," he replied. "She's had no daughters of her own, so she's not used to young, pretty girls being around the place."

"Their younger son told me that their dad lived with another woman for a few years."

"So, he's cheated on Gloria," he said. "Well, it's

not going to do you any good to get caught up in their marital problems."

"I know," I replied.

"I've got to get back to work," Daniel said suddenly.

I panicked inside at the thought of being on my own again. But I didn't want to show my anxiety, so I smiled at Daniel, and said, "Can we meet up again for lunch next week?"

"Sure thing," and he smiled warmly.

After I'd picked up the dry-cleaning, I went into a café, ordered a coffee, and sat down at a table. I tried to read my book, but I couldn't concentrate. Feeling in a panic, I now rang my mum.

"Hello, mum," I said.

"What is it, Emily?" my mum said sharply. She was in her office, and she seemed annoyed to be interrupted.

"I've got to move out. I really hate the job," I blurted. "I can't do the cooking."

"Well you should have thought of that before you took the job," she said.

"I need some money to move out," I said.

"I'm not bailing you out this time," my mum snapped.

I hunched over my coffee, utterly deflated. "So, what am I supposed to do?"

"You'll have to save up some money," she said firmly. "Look, I've got work to get on with. Goodbye," and she put down the phone abruptly.

I felt numb. *Why didn't she understand?* Our relationship had gone from bad to worse in the last few weeks. Though I'd spoken to Mum on the phone a few times recently, when we usually fell out, I hadn't actually seen her since I'd taken the nanny job a couple of months ago. Like Granny, she had pressurised me into taking this job, even when I expressed doubt about it, when I was packing my things at my previous landlady's to move here. I hadn't even seen my mum at Christmas, as I didn't want to stay at Granny's house, because I knew that I would be criticised by both of them about not seeming able to stick at any job.

What if I sold my cello? It was the only possession I had which was valuable. I knew that it was worth several thousand pounds. I remembered that Grandpa had bought the cello from a lady who had kept it in her attic, and hadn't known its true value. It was a French Bavarian cello, dated 1830. Its back was new, as many years ago it had been dropped down the stairs, but it still had a beautiful tone. My mum had learned on this instrument at the Royal College of Music when she was a teenager. Then I had played it between the ages of nine and eighteen, when I had stopped because my back pain made practice so painful, as did carrying the instrument up the hill to orchestra practice at university. Even so, I didn't want to sell my cello.

That evening, back in my room, I took the cello out of its case and tried to play it.

There was a knock on the door and Gloria came straight in. "Could you stop that? The children's PE kits need to be washed, and their bags need to be packed for school tomorrow," she said sharply.

She was a slim, attractive woman in her early fifties, with curly, long, dyed blonde hair, and lively blue eyes. She was very assertive, and had a stage presence about her, which reminded me that she had enjoyed a successful career as a dancer until she had her children late on.

"Well, I won't be playing the cello much more," I replied abruptly. "I'm selling it."

"You don't need to do that." But as she said this, her eyes shot me a mean look.

"Yes, I do, I need the money," I mumbled. I didn't add *to move out*, but that was what I said to myself in my head.

Gloria closed the door. I sighed, and packed away the cello. I found being around the boys stressful now, with Gloria criticising me if I made any mistake with the cooking. I often hid how I felt, as I didn't want to get into an argument with her. As much as I now hated the job, I couldn't risk getting fired, when I had nowhere to go.

Seven

Gloria now gave me so many chores that I had no time to leave the flat until late in the evening. I would try to stay calm, but when I finally got out of the flat I'd be furious, as usually I'd be late to meet my friends. This left two hours, at the most, to chat with my friends over a glass or two of wine before I had to leave. I needed to be awake and out of bed early in the morning to get the oldest boy up for school.

My friends Beth and Sarah I had known since sixth form, and both were living and working in London. But often I couldn't relax, because even with them I'd sometimes hear the men's voices, or the spiteful female voice. I was convinced I'd lose them as friends if they knew. So I took care to hide how frightened I felt at the voices. Inevitably, I looked tense and preoccupied as I struggled to cope. I even took to drinking more wine in an effort to calm myself. One evening on the way home I bought a bottle of whiskey and sneaked it into the flat in my bag; I hid it in my wardrobe, and locked the door. I told myself that if I really couldn't sleep, I would drink a glass of whiskey, as I didn't want to go to the doctor to get sleeping pills.

I felt relief when the cooking seemed to go better for a while. I needed to feel a sense of control over what I was doing. I knew that much about myself.

But I couldn't escape the voices. I retreated to the nearby café to read, whenever I could, but this was futile.

"I thought she wouldn't come out," shouted the brittle male voice. His tone was nasty.

"Maybe she needs to find out," shouted an older male voice.

Find out what? I looked up at the window to see a young woman passing. So where were they? There was more shouting, as the cars sped past. Were the woman and the men further down the street, out of sight? I felt oddly disorientated.

I had to go and see for myself what these voices behind the wall really were. I grabbed my coat. It was chilly outside. Cars were passing, and as they rushed past me the voices became louder. I could still hear each voice separately - and as more cars passed, they became a deafening roar.

"She fancies herself," said the female voice spitefully.

"Is that it?" shouted the older male voice.

"We're looking at her now," roared the brittle male voice.

This made me very afraid again. These people were talking about me. I didn't like that. So I walked up the crowded street to search for the voices, but I didn't find them. Then I turned down a quiet side street. I could still hear the voices. Were the woman and men on the corner of the road? I wanted to shout out, who are you? But what if these were ordinary voices? People might think I'm crazy.

A short while later, when I was back at the flat loading the dishwasher, I couldn't make up my mind whether I needed to call a friend. I had my mobile in my bag. I wasn't sure if I could ring for help. It was quiet in the flat, as the family were visiting one of Gloria's relatives.

"I thought she wouldn't come back here," the man with the brittle voice was saying.

"She needs to make an effort," the other man replied.

Then I stared abruptly at the wall. These voices seemed to project through the wall. *These men were in the other room, surely?* Had Gloria asked them to come round, because she wanted me to be scared, so that I would leave? The voices now teased me. But I was too frightened to leave the kitchen. The voices had been joined by the spiteful female voice, who was saying, "She's not getting on with things." It was the sort of thing that my mum might have said. I now felt angry, and started to argue with the female voice.

I was so distracted by this argument that I still hadn't set the table for dinner when the family returned. Gloria looked upset, but she didn't scold me as I was expecting. Instead, she was quiet. Then I turned crimson, realising that she might have overheard me talking to the people. I now imagined myself shrunk to a tiny dot on the wall, as I didn't want to be in this kitchen any longer.

The dinner that evening with the two boys seemed to go on for ever. We ate meat pies, with carrots and asparagus. Gloria sat with us, which was not usual, and I felt panicky as I tried to follow their words. I could still hear the men's voices talking next door, and it was very distracting. They were now picking on my back surgery, which I had undergone two years earlier.

A memory flooded my mind of the dull pain that I'd experienced day in and day out after the operation.

"Her surgeon said that she wasn't born with the problem. Something happened," the man with the brittle voice was saying.

"She won't say what it is," the other man replied.

"Well, she knows," the female voice said suddenly.

What was this? An interrogation? With nothing to explain these voices picking away at me, I felt very tense.

I looked abruptly at Gloria, wondering if she could hear the voices as well. But then, when I had searched for these voices earlier in the street, I hadn't seen anyone. Yet somehow it seemed that people were really there.

I wished that I could escape from the kitchen, but there was still the table to clear, the dishwasher to load, the boys' schoolbags to pack for tomorrow, and their PE kits to sort.

The boys got up and went through to the playroom to watch telly. Gloria stepped towards me, looking thoughtful. I was expecting her to criticise how I had slightly burnt the pies for dinner. "Emily, I'm concerned about you," she said firmly. "Are you hearing voices?"

"No!" I insisted. "I don't hear voices. Earlier I was talking to a friend on my phone."

But her concerned expression remained, and I sensed that she didn't believe me. "Nigel hears voices, and he talks to them," she said. She had a serious-looking face, as if this was no joke.

I didn't believe her. I thought that she had made this up to trick me into saying that I heard voices too. She must think I was really crazy.

By the time Friday came, I had burnt some lasagne in the oven, and Gloria said afterwards, "I told you that this was your last chance. We can't have you here any longer. Burning the boys' dinner is unacceptable."

"But I've improved at the cooking. Please give me another chance," I begged.

"Sorry, you need to leave. Having you here isn't good for you or for the boys," she replied.

I'd already lost the job, I knew it. So I passively stared back at her, holding back the tears that pricked my eyes. No job. No home. What was I going to do?

"She's a failure, she always is," said the brittle, clipped voice in an angry tone.

I felt shaky. Was this all a nightmare? Or was I really a crazy person, who just couldn't get it together?

Nigel was kinder to me that evening, when he met me in the corridor. "D'you have somewhere to go?" he asked me.

I didn't want to look pathetic. "Yes, I'll sort something out," I replied.

I still couldn't believe my situation. "I think she makes no effort," the man with the nasal, brittle voice was saying. Despite hearing the voice, I knew that I had to call Tim, a friend from university, to see if I could stay with him for a while until I could get a job again.

Two hours later, I had managed to get hold of Tim, and he was happy for me to take all my things there and crash in his room for a while. In any case, he was working in America for the next month, so it would be just his brother living in the flat with me.

But I'd become so distressed that I struggled even to pack up my things. So when Daniel came round to put my suitcases in a taxi, not everything was packed.

"She's got men running round after her," Gloria said nastily as we walked past her down the corridor towards the front door.

I waited until we were out of earshot, then I turned to Daniel, and said, "Did you hear that?"

He was struggling to carry two heavy suitcases, and he said, "Just ignore her. She's a bitch."

But his words didn't make me feel much better. Anyway, I still had to work until the end of the week.

For the next couple of days, I stayed in my room whenever I could. On a couple of occasions their older son brought me a cup of tea. I didn't know if Nigel had asked him to do this. Exhaustion, and whiskey, pushed me into sleep - my only escape from the misery of my situation.

By the time my last morning arrived, I still didn't have everything packed, so I had no choice but to relay this fact to Nigel.

"You can't stay here tonight," he said firmly.

"What about my things?"

"We'll have them delivered to your friend's

address, if you write it down," he said, and he handed me a notepad.

So I got my diary, and scribbled down the address on the notepad. I went back to my room, and there was a knock on the door. Gloria entered and said, "I don't want to end it on a bad note. I'm sorry that it hasn't worked out. I hope things go well for you."

"What? You've cracked me up by criticising me non-stop," I said angrily. I wanted to let her know what I really thought of her before I left.

Gloria's face was mask-like. I couldn't tell what she was thinking, but she certainly didn't look upset as she shut the door.

"Did you hear that?" said a man's voice in a concerned tone. It sounded as if it was Nigel speaking. He could be in the corridor, couldn't he?

I grabbed my coat and bag. I saw Nigel near the front door, and he said, "Good luck."

I felt I owed him some kind of explanation, but I couldn't think of one. So I just forced a smile and said, "Goodbye." Then I was leaving through the open front door.

Out in the corridor of the flats it was really chilly. I wrapped my scarf more tightly round my neck and got in the lift to go downstairs. I was a student, not a crazy person; why didn't I feel that? As the lift reached the ground floor, I felt more frantic and scared, particularly as the voices had started again.

I didn't want to go on the Underground, but there wasn't much choice. I thought that if I reached the British Museum I might feel better, because I could enjoy looking at the Roman statues there, and relax over a coffee.

Since I was frightened by the voices, I stood back

from the platform edge as the train drew in, and got on board feeling shaky. The voices were screaming at me from the next train carriage. I kept careful watch whenever anyone entered or left the train, in case the people that the voices belonged to came on board.

"We're losing contact with her," the man with the brittle voice was saying.

I was relieved to reach the museum finally, but even there the voices didn't stop. I was worried that Tim's brother would be freaked out by me if I arrived at the flat looking agitated, so I was determined to calm down. Despite having told Tim of my plan to stay there tonight, I knew that it was flexible what time I arrived. As the voices kept echoing in the large museum, I decided that I would go round to Tim's flat earlier, as he had left his key under a flowerpot for me. And as hard as it was to put on a good face, this was better than crumbling under the pressure of the voices.

Eight

On the way to the flat I picked up the ingredients to make spaghetti bolognese for myself and Tim's brother, Ed. I thought that if we ate dinner together, that would be a good ice-breaker as I hadn't met Ed before. I was determined to cope as best I could, by keeping conversation light and easy so that he didn't guess about the voices. The last thing I wanted was for him to think I was crazy.

I would later think that my effort that night to keep myself steady was superb; it was my stubbornness and perfectionist trait, as I didn't want to be beaten by the fear of the voices. Ed was delighted that I had cooked him a dinner, and I cracked some jokes and laughed, and was pleased when Ed did the same.

But I had other frightening experiences as well. That night it was as if the voices were talking about me above my head in the flat upstairs. Through the window I watched shadows moving in the wind. I listened again to the voices. I was very frightened, as I now believed that the voices belonged to people who were stalking me.

I was so petrified that I went to knock on Ed's door, and said, "Could you come into my room. I'm too scared to sleep on my own."

"Is it a nightmare?" he asked me.

"Something like that," I replied.

Ed was very tall, and though quiet, I could tell he was assertive. I felt some comfort knowing that he was with me. My terror was all encompassing, and I didn't consider for a moment that Ed might think that I was trying to make a move on him.

But the next evening when he came in, it was obvious that he was embarrassed by the previous night, and I struggled for the right thing to say as an explanation for how afraid I had been.

Ed now said, "I spoke to Tim on the phone. He thinks we need to have a plan for how we can sort out the problem that you were having last night."

"Oh really," I said hesitantly.

I now wondered if Tim had told Ed about my mental health problem. Tim had seen me in a very distressed state in my college room in York when I was drunk, convinced that I was going to fail my degree. But at that point I hadn't been hearing voices.

Ed was looking concerned.

"I have a health problem... Well, it's my mental health," I said reluctantly. "I think I need to see a doctor." I studied Ed's face, but he didn't look shocked.

"There's King's College Hospital round the corner," he said. "Let's go there, so that you can see a doctor." His tone was kind.

"I need to work again, so I've got to get better," I

said. But I was worrying now about the stigma, so I added, “My mental health problem doesn't make me a psychopath.”

Ed laughed, and said, “I didn't think you were one.”

I was relieved to have his help, for the voices were commenting on me again. I couldn't bear having these voices spying on me and judging me any longer. I thought that it was a lucky coincidence that we were going to King’s College Hospital, as this was the hospital where I'd been born.

In the small room in the Accident and Emergency department at King’s College Hospital, I worried about the nasty, brittle voice that was now picking on me. I had mentioned that I suffered from bipolar disorder to a doctor, and I was now waiting for a psychiatrist to see me. I was on my own, as I had asked Ed to wait for me in the main reception area.

I wasn't sure what help the doctor would be. But then I listened again to the voices. They seemed to project through the wall. I wondered again if men were actually there. Maybe the doctor could help me?

The doctor who pulled back the green curtain was tall, slim and good-looking, with spiky brown hair and a kind face. He looked as if he was in his thirties.

“Hello, I'm Dr Phillips. How can I help you?” He seemed open and approachable.

“I was diagnosed a few years ago as bipolar, but recently I've been hearing voices,” I blurted out.

I expected him to flinch when he heard this. But his expression remained calm and neutral. “Have you been under any stress lately?" he asked me.

"I've just been fired from an au pair job that I hated," I said. "The woman kept picking on me, because I kept making mistakes with the cooking. I stopped sleeping at night, and that was when I began hearing the voices."

Suddenly again the older and wiser voice, and the brittle, clipped voice were there. I didn't like the idea of these voices listening in to my conversation with the doctor.

"Stress can cause you to hear voices," said the psychiatrist. "Under a lot of pressure you can have what we call a 'brief psychotic episode'."

"Does it mean I'm crazy?" I suggested.

"No, there are some pills that will help," he said. "Do you feel like harming yourself?"

"No," I replied.

"Do you think that you are a risk to anyone else?" he asked me.

"No...of course not," I replied, feeling alarmed that he had asked this. He must think that I really was crazy. "I need to get a new job, so I can earn some money," I said. I thought that if I mentioned work I would look more normal.

"Well, I'll sort out some prescriptions for you," said the psychiatrist. "Are you here with your friend?"

"He's my friend's brother," I replied.

"Is it all right if I talk to him?" asked the psychiatrist.

I didn't like the idea of Ed knowing too many details, so I shook my head. "I don't know him that well," I said.

"Well, I'll tell you what, there's a number I can

give you in case you have any difficulties over the next few days."

So I took the prescriptions he gave me, and went out to the waiting room to join Ed.

"You okay?" he asked me, grinning.

"Yes, I got some prescriptions," I replied. "I'll be all right now."

He looked relieved, as if he had been struggling with the idea of how to help someone who thought they had gone crazy. I felt guilty at asking for his help, but also relieved that my problem of hearing voices had been shared.

Over the next week I spent most of my time on the internet searching for a job. I had to make and return calls; I had no time to read books or spend time writing. The pills made me feel slightly deadened and numb, but at least I could sleep at night. After getting a couple of nights of good sleep I stopped taking the pills, as I felt more positive and the voices had faded away altogether.

The next afternoon I received a text from Gloria saying that she was having my things delivered. I went outside to find a pile of black bin-liners next to the front door. I really wished that Ed was here, but I was on my own. So I struggled to carry the heavy sacks into the flat. I checked through them, hoping that everything was there. To my surprise in the bottom of my rucksack I found a green-eyed copper cat, and a green and silver silky thong. Did these belong to Gloria? I felt so upset that I called my friend Beth.

"How's everything?" she asked me.

"It could be better," I replied. "Gloria's just dumped my stuff round here in bin-liners," I said.

"In one of the bags is a copper cat and her thong."

"Oh, gross! That sounds like bad karma," Beth replied. "How mean of her."

"I know," I replied. Had Gloria thought that I was jealous of her? I felt uneasy now, thinking that a stretch of bad luck was going to follow.

I needed to get work. Later that week, I was offered a short-term teaching job by Anne-Marie, the headmistress of a primary school in an expensive part of Chelsea. I had recently tutored her daughter for A-level History, and she had gained an A grade in the exam. Anne-Marie partly credited me with this success, so now she was confident that I could fill in for the Head of English, who was on sick leave while she recovered from an operation. Anne-Marie described this job as 'babysitting the classes' while this teacher was away.

The private school was all-girls, in a Victorian converted red brick house. I started out getting to the school early in the mornings to prepare my lessons on handwriting and creative writing. The classes were small, with well-behaved girls, who ranged in age from seven to eleven. For the first three weeks I did manage the busy timetable, even helping other teachers to take the whole school on a trip to the London Eye. I didn't feel too stressed, though at break-times I was relieved to be cocooned in the staffroom with the other teachers, to do my paperwork. For when I stood in front of a class, I had to put on a performance as if I were an actress.

But in the fourth week, I slipped behind with the marking. Getting up very early in the morning put me under more pressure, and in the evenings when I was tired I began to hear the brittle, clipped voice again, and the neutral man's voice discussing me. Mostly they gave broken commentaries, picking on things that I had done during the day; just a phrase here and there.

It didn't help that one afternoon my mum rang me on my mobile while I was in the classroom doing some marking. She kept asking me nosy questions about where I was living, and my new job, and we got into a row. That's when I saw Anne-Marie, the headmistress, watching from the shadow of the hallway. I didn't like the idea of her listening to me. Embarrassed, I quickly finished the call.

A couple of days later, Anne-Marie crossed the classroom to speak to me, with a kind smile. It was Friday lunchtime, and I was planning some lessons.

“Thank you for what you've done to help me, Emily,” she said. “But I've noticed that you've got behind with marking the books. So I think it's time I asked Mrs Thorpe to come back. She’s one of our very experienced teachers, who does supply work. I would have said something before, but this matter only came to my attention in the last day or two.”

I wanted to cry, but instead I gave her one of my tight-lipped smiles.

Anne-Marie said, “If there's anything worrying you, please come over to my house, and we can have a chat over a cup of tea. I’ll be in this evening, and you'd be very welcome.”

“Thanks,” I said. When she left, I immediately started to pack my bag, as I was anxious to leave.

I remember that the brittle voice that I sometimes heard became nasty and more intrusive then. I heard him talking to me as I left the school, even though I was carrying an enormous bouquet of colourful flowers that had been given to me as a leaving present.

I didn't feel like stopping at Anne-Marie's house for a chat and a cup of tea. I reckoned this invitation was to go into the reasons why I'd lost the job, and whether these played on my mind. I didn't want to challenge her decision to ask me to leave, as I liked Anne-Marie, and I also knew that I wasn't a trained teacher. Years later, I now realise that Anne-Marie must have had concerns about my mental health, and saw me as a vulnerable young woman. She had daughters of my age, and I imagine she wanted to offer me a safe place to find help. She had overheard the conversation with my mum, and perhaps she sensed that my relationship with my family was not good. But at that time, I couldn't see that people were worried about me, and on the Tube home I felt angry and alone. I was only cheered up by the bouquet of flowers that I was holding, that people kept noticing.

So there was another job hunt, and I had to move out of Tim's bedroom as he'd come back from America with a new girlfriend. I left the flat on good terms with Tim and Ed. I had earned a generous amount of money at the school, so I was able to find a room in a house in Fulham, which was close to where my friend Beth lived. I didn't want to teach classes of children any longer, because I found this stressful. So I found a job in a school near Oxford Street, teaching English as a Foreign Language through basic conversation skills to the Muslim wives of Saudi Arabian embassy officials. But the money was not enough to cover my rent and living expenses, so I got extra tutoring in the evenings, going into offices to teach Business English to Japanese businessmen and French investment bankers. I found all the travelling from Fulham exhausting, and yet I still had sleepless nights, so I would drink whiskey to try to get to sleep.

I was working so hard during these four months that I had little time left to see my friends. In the evenings I often heard voices, and it actually felt safe to be cocooned in my flat, to unwind with a bottle of wine. But as my social life shrank away, some new voices started in earnest.

It was in early June that I looked up from my desk where I was planning my lessons: I could hear voices coming from the other side of the wall. I thought they must be the men collecting the rubbish from the bins. But it was after ten in the evening, and pitch dark outside. I felt so afraid that I reached again for the whiskey bottle, and topped up my glass. I listened to the brittle, clipped voice saying, “She's borderline, it's cruel.” I found this really upsetting, so I started to write this poem:

Borderline

Border states.
Choosing realities,
No shape at all.

Shape size shape.
Border knock down,

Flood in attention to self.
Borders - shut down.
Cut out by rulers - again,
Occupied. Occupied.
Stave reality. Gone gone away.
Border-border states.

There it was down on the page. I realised that I was keeping myself 'occupied' by working hard, to drive away the voices. The people were chattering again, and being really nasty about me. I now decided that I couldn't face going into college the next morning, and instead I would finish the bottle of whiskey so I could sleep.

Nine

All that week, I stayed in my flat with the door locked. A part of me was paranoid too. The people kept chattering about me. Sometimes their tone was ambivalent, neutral. I couldn't make up my mind whether they were being unkind or not.

I had bought myself several bottles of wine and I kept topping up my glass, as I wanted everything to feel less painful. The voices were dulled by the wine, but still somehow it seemed that people were really there.

A few days later my paranoia had escalated. The voices seemed to project through the ceiling. I thought that my landlord and landlady were talking about me upstairs, and I strained to listen.

"She makes no effort," the man with the brittle voice was saying.

"I'm very concerned," the other man replied.

"I think she should kill herself," said the woman suddenly. She said it in a persuasive tone, as if this might be a good idea.

I stared ahead at the beige wall, wondering if she was right. I had wanted to make a difference in my life, but now my attempts at achieving something had all failed. Didn't women of my age have jobs and partners? And they didn't feel frightened all the time. I started to cry as I reached for a pen. I wanted to write a final note to Daniel, and then another note to my mum, explaining why I was going to kill myself.

Incredibly, I didn't take an overdose that afternoon as I'd planned. I did post the suicide notes, but a need for self-preservation kicked in, and I continued down the road to my favourite coffee shop. The voices kept chattering away in nasty tones. I couldn't face returning alone to my flat, so I spoke on the phone to Granny. She encouraged me to catch a train to her house. I went to the station and bought a ticket. I must have looked very distressed, for a young man travelling on the same train said, "Are you okay?"

"Yes, thanks," I said, my words slightly slurred, for I had been drinking wine all afternoon.

When I arrived at Granny's house, she gave me a warm, firm hug, and said, "I'm so glad that you're here, Emily. Things will get better, trust me." She gave me her special smile.

Tears welled up in my eyes at that moment, and I couldn't hold them back. "I've gone crazy. Everything is wrong," I blurted out. Still, I didn't tell Granny about the voices. I knew that she couldn't protect me from these people who kept talking about me, and I felt afraid. "Can you call Mum and ask her to come over?" I asked Granny.

Granny nodded. "I'll call her right now," she said.

My mum came over within half an hour, and was surprised when I turned to her for comfort, curling up next to her on the settee and sobbing. She sat next to me stiffly. I sensed that she didn't know what to say. It must have been very concerning for my mum and Granny to witness my mental distress.

"I keep losing jobs," I sobbed. "At the au pair job I was just their skivvy. That's when the voices started."

"That was very naughty of them," said Granny. "If they knew that you came from a nice family, they probably would have treated you differently."

My mum clearly was alarmed by my distress, and she phoned an out-of-hours number for the GP surgery. She took me to the Accident and Emergency department of the local hospital. Once again I was seen by a psychiatrist, only this time I was admitted to a psychiatric ward. That night I was given a powerful sedative that immediately put me into a deep sleep.

The next day Granny arrived to visit me. She was stooped over her 'pushy', a semi-frame on wheels that helped her to walk. I felt relieved to see a friendly face.

"You look brighter today," she said, giving me a hug. "I'm sure that in no time at all we'll have you feeling better. You're in the right place to be helped."

I wasn't as convinced, but I managed to force a smile. The voices were chattering again.

We were in the lounge area of the ward, which was nearly empty. Just then a male nurse walked in, and said, "Emily, we're going to transfer you to a hospital in London, as we don't have a bed here."

I gained some strength from having Granny there,

and now the thought of being moved miles away made me frightened. But the hospital's attitude was that where I was going to be treated had already been decided.

Not only was I transported by ambulance that afternoon to the hospital, but on the ward they took away my phone charger and the cord of the dressing gown that my mum had lent me. They clearly thought that I posed a danger to myself.

I was given a mood stabiliser medication, but I still couldn't stop the voices. They seemed to project through the walls of the hospital. The neutral, male voice suddenly sounded like a doctor, who in an authoritative way discussed whether I would be better diagnosed as 'bipolar' or 'schizophrenic'. I found this very upsetting, but I didn't trust any of the nurses enough to tell them this. I didn't want to be labelled as 'schizophrenic', did I?

I felt so distressed in the night that I lay awake, and that's when I heard voices on the roof, from the people I believed were stalking me. They were picking on me in the way that I described earlier on.

One of the nurses told me the next morning that I'd be meeting with a social worker. I remembered my experience of meeting with a female social worker many years before: she had talked to me at school and then placed me in foster-care that afternoon, without calling my grandparents. I felt paranoid that this new social worker would also intervene in a way that I didn't want.

The middle-aged, bald social worker promised to help. But when I asked him for leave from the ward to go to the shops, this was met with his and the nurses' stony faces shaking 'no'.

I didn't like the idea of staying stuck on a ward, where there was even a net covering the outdoor area with its picnic benches. Just a week earlier I had been working full-time as a teacher. It seemed so long ago now.

"There's no pressure to go back to work," said the social worker. "You can claim medium to long-term benefits. We can help with that."

"Will those benefits cover my rent?" I asked him.

"Yes, there's housing benefit," he replied.

I remember feeling relieved, but at the same time worried. Did this mean that they thought I was so mentally ill that I couldn't work again for a very long time? It wasn't that I wasn't trying - I just couldn't cope with the voices. What if these voices were here to stay? In thirty years' time I'd be like the grey, overweight mentally ill women on the ward, who sat zonked out in front of daytime telly. This thought terrified me.

Ten

It felt strange being out of hospital, after five weeks staying there. I felt ashamed that I had crossed the line from being a teacher to being a psychiatric patient. I also didn't have an income now, or the structure to my day that work had provided. Summer had arrived, but I didn't enjoy taking sunny, leafy walks: I preferred to sit cocooned in my favourite café writing poems and drinking cappuccinos. The poems frequently reflected how I felt, as I was still very troubled by the voices.

In the café, I got chatting to an elderly man with a moustache, who was often reading books. He was a psychologist, and smoked a pipe, which made me think of Freud. One morning after a very public row with my mum on the phone, he said, "You look very distressed."

"I'm never going to work again. I had a breakdown this summer," I said.

He didn't look afraid. "People do recover from breakdowns," he said, and smiled.

I had been awake since early morning with the

voices picking on me, so I added, “Not if they hear voices.”

“Certainly, hearing a voice can be a problem. But that too is something you can learn to cope with,” he replied.

I didn’t believe him. I watched as he went outside to smoke his pipe.

Apart from speaking to this man, and sometimes meeting up with Beth or Daniel, who were both very supportive, I didn’t arrange to see anyone. I didn’t want to visit my friends from university, not even Tim and Ed, as they all had jobs, and I felt ashamed of the fact that I wasn’t working. I became increasingly isolated and withdrawn.

I did have some follow-up appointments with a social worker at the Community Mental Health Team. He wasn’t the bald man I had previously seen at the hospital, but a younger, easy-going man, who did his best to make me feel better about my current situation. “Don’t put yourself under pressure at the moment. It takes time to recover,” he kept saying.

But I felt despair. I kept a journal at that time, and here is one of my entries.

8 August

I don't even want to occupy my ‘ego’ – that is my strength. I made the decision to give it up over 10 years ago. I never want to become a person again, so I intend to play with this ‘hell’ I have as my ‘ego’. I intend to use it in a creative fashion for my writing, and I'm not going to become intimidated by what are essentially facets of my own character.

I felt that I had to mention the voices to the psychiatrist, and an anti-psychotic medication was prescribed. I never shared my journal with anyone, but I did post my poems to Daniel, who said that he was happy for me to do this. I thought that I needed an audience for the overwhelming feelings that I was expressing, so that I wasn't alone with these. The biggest hurdle at this time was the isolation, and I could really have benefited at this point from a referral to an Early Psychosis Team that might have invited me to some social activities for young people who were recovering from a psychotic episode; but this didn't happen. I didn't know any other young person who also experienced psychosis, so I didn't know that recovery was possible.

The psychiatrist did refer me for cognitive behavioural therapy with a clinical psychologist who worked in the hospital. When I met with a grey-haired psychologist called Peter, he smiled at me reassuringly. During the session, I was encouraged to say what was on my mind, but all the time I worried about mentioning the voices. I already felt blunted and sleepy from the medication, so I didn't want this increased, which would happen if the staff still thought that I had 'symptoms'.

During one session, Peter did manage to get me to identify a feeling of worthlessness that now affected my ability to stick with achieving anything that I planned to do. On a whiteboard, Peter had drawn a pair of measuring scales, and written 'evidence for' and 'evidence against'. He said, "In what way do your voices support this feeling that you're worthless?"

I actively recoiled from this mention of the voices.

"My voices tell me I'm stupid," I replied reluctantly.

"What is the evidence for this?" he asked me, still holding his pen.

I shrugged, and said, "I didn't finish my PGCE."

"That's not a good measure of being stupid," he replied, smiling. "Not many people are qualified teachers."

So, he's another of the mental health professionals who wants me to lower my expectations of what I can achieve, I thought to myself.

Peter was now writing on his clipboard; I felt frustrated and angry, and shrank back in my seat.

I was only allotted twelve sessions of cognitive behavioural therapy, and two of these I missed because I overslept. I didn't find helpful the diagrams that Peter drew on his whiteboard, and I'd postpone doing the homework exercises he gave me, particularly those that focused on the voices.

In fact, any expression of what I was feeling – fear, boredom, depression, despair – I didn't want to mention to him. Then, in a later session, he suggested to me that I was on the autistic spectrum. *So, I've got no social skills as well,* I thought to myself. Too polite to say this, I listened to Peter talking about 'Aspies' (for Asperger's), who he claimed welcomed the fact that they were different.

When Peter had to leave the room briefly to speak to someone, I flicked through my file, and there I saw my diagnosis – *schizoaffective disorder.* 'Schizo', like the murderers and nutters who made headline news for committing violent, anti-social crimes. I recoiled in horror.

The door was opening, and I hastily pushed back the file. Peter said, "Sorry about that interruption. Now, let's get back to what we were talking about – "

I stared back, resolving to say very little in the remaining sessions with him.

Depressed at this new diagnosis, I got drunk after the session finished, as a way of trying to escape my emotional pain.

I spent a difficult Christmas with my family, being very withdrawn. I withdrew to my bedroom at Granny's house, secretly drinking wine and writing poems as a way of trying to distract myself from the voices, which made Granny and my Aunt Janis very concerned about me. I was encouraged by my aunt to return to Fulham, but I didn't leave Granny's house for a few weeks. By then the voices had turned really nasty, and feeling very paranoid I sought refuge again in the hospital.

This time a different anti-psychotic medication was tried, but the voices persisted. The medication made me pile on the pounds. I had been proud of my slim figure, so as I ballooned, I lost confidence and became more depressed.

I still kept on writing. I often felt too paranoid to write in the café, so I was pleased when my social worker referred me to a mental health centre; he told me it had rooms where I could do my creative writing and play the piano.

A one-storey, red brick building, the centre was a bus-ride from where I lived, in a run-down area, and sometimes it got vandalised or broken into. Nevertheless, I found the place to be a refuge. I believed that in the centre I'd be protected from the voices, because the people couldn't follow me in there. This never struck me as delusional thinking, because I'd split off the voices as being separate from me.

When I was offered a cup of tea by a mental health worker and sat down with the service-users, who were playing Bingo, I felt a fragile joy and great relief: I was not alone.

I really liked one of the service-users, Lenny: he was an elderly man, a Russian Jewish immigrant. For many years he had worked as a labourer on the roads. At the centre he kept himself occupied with drawing portraits, which he made by carefully copying photographs that people had given him of relatives or their pets. He told me that at the age of twenty-five he'd 'cracked up' one day at work. Hearing the voice of 'the Devil' commanding him to 'kill himself', he'd gone to his foreman in tears and told him, "I need to go home."

His foreman had replied, "Don't worry, Lenny. There was a time I couldn't leave my home."

Lenny told me that this implied to him that his foreman had experienced mental illness. Lenny respected his foreman, because he was a very strong man, who had been a Jarrow marcher. He'd marched from Durham to London to protest that he and his men needed work.

I envied Lenny having this experience of receiving compassion and understanding in the workplace; whereas I'd recently gone from job to job, feeling I needed to lie about my problem with the voices.

Lenny was a good listener, and I was gradually able to share with him the struggle that I was still having with the voices, and how desperate and lonely this made me feel.

Lenny shook his head. He said, “Mine was like burning electric acid in my brain. The first thought I had on waking in the morning was about getting back to bed that night. But I’d go to work and battle all day, hearing the Devil’s voice. I was so ill that I had to work, because it was a way of battling it. The Devil was there from the moment I woke up to the time I lay my head down to sleep. It was 24/7.”

“Do you still hear the voice now?” I asked him.

“Not much now,” he replied. “I'd say it burned itself out over the years.” His tone was calm, and certainly the relaxed expression on his face suggested to me that he'd found some peace. I felt encouraged, knowing that someone else's struggle with their voice had ceased.

With days of unemployment stretching ahead, I got into a pattern of taking a bag of books with me to the centre in the mornings; but mostly I sat chatting with the other service-users, who were mainly middle-aged and elderly people who had spent a long time in the mental health system. Often they talked about how unwell they felt, and about what psychiatric medications they were taking, comparing dosages. These conversations circled in my head, and I now viewed myself as being genuinely mentally ill.

The centre did arrange activities, and sometimes I had a foot massage or a piano lesson, or joined in the art class or newspaper discussion group. And then there were the outings to local museums and to the parks. I walked with the other service-users feeling ashamed, for mental illness comes with a terrible stigma – and I knew that I didn't want to look like 'one of them'. I'd learned an unpleasant lesson on a day trip with the centre to an art gallery in London. One of the museum assistants said to one of our support workers, "Are they all retarded?"

The support worker looked angry, and she snapped, "No, they're not. Could I speak to you in private?" They moved away to a corner of the gallery, so I didn't get to hear what was said next.

So I judged myself harshly for spending so much time with the other service-users. I now realise that I had internalized the stigma that exists in society towards the mentally ill. Not only were they viewed by some people as having learning disabilities, but they were also seen as unpredictable and potentially violent. Over the years that followed, one of my biggest struggles was that I stigmatised myself. I had to work hard not to project this onto others who were visibly mentally ill, or I'd stigmatise them as well.

During this time I met up with my mum once a fortnight: we'd eat a salad in an Italian restaurant, then go for a drive round Richmond Park. We often argued, and sometimes my mum would forget the speed bumps in the road, positioned to slow down the cars passing through the grey deer that grazed in the park. Before, our relationship had involved challenges because she envied the fact that I'd grown up with my grandparents, while she needed to be out earning money because my father paid no child maintenance. But now she couldn't comprehend my reluctance to find work, or engage in activities that I'd previously enjoyed. Coming from a high-achieving family, my mum, like Granny, placed tremendous value on exam results and one's professional career.

"You don't understand," I screamed at her in the car. "I'm not who I was before I cracked up. I now hear voices when I'm stressed. They say horrible things, like 'I'm stupid and nobody loves me'."

"That's not true," said my mum quickly. But her face looked crushed.

"Isn't it? I don't have a boyfriend, do I?" I cried. "Who's going to go out with me now I'm so fat?" I rarely slept with Daniel now, as he didn't seem to fancy me any more. He preferred slim women. I'd been put on a different anti-psychotic medication, so that I wouldn't gain more weight. But I hadn't been able to lose any weight either.

"Part of the problem is that you don't make any effort to meet a boyfriend," replied Mum.

The car scraped across another bump, and Mum swore. I slumped further back into my seat, feeling bitter and disappointed that I couldn't get her to see my perspective.

So the months passed, and my identity as a mental patient stuck with me, as I fulfilled the low expectations which mental health staff held for me. Daniel had encouraged me to start tutoring again, and I did find myself a few students to tutor. But as soon as the voices became difficult, I gradually reduced my number of students until I only taught two boys. Their mum was a clinical psychologist, and I would feel paranoid if she found out that I had a diagnosis; but week after week she was welcoming and pleased with the boys' progress, so I kept going back to their home to give lessons.

In October, I even started a Master's in History and Archaeology at Birkbeck College, as I was very drawn to studying Roman history, in particular the old cities of Roman Britain. When I lived in Canterbury, I had enjoyed exploring a sunken Roman house that had mosaic floors. But while I did read the coursebooks, the travelling proved a nightmare, as the voices screamed at me from the next carriage when I was on the Tube. A part of me felt paranoid that other passengers were staring at me, as I was now officially 'the crazy woman', as much as I tried to pretend otherwise. I worried that I'd react and shout back at the voices of the people who I believed were stalking me. What if I lost control, and was violent? Years later, I realise that these illusions of persecution were worsened by the fact that I usually had rather a lot of alcohol in my bloodstream. I had such low self-esteem that I started dating a manipulative man who would embarrass me in front of other students in the college bar by kissing me passionately and running his hands over my breasts. I would be drinking wine, and I didn't care enough to tell him to stop. I lasted less than a term on the course before I quit.

I was fortunate in that some kind people did try to help. The lady who taught me the piano at the centre was very accepting of my difficulties. When I was hung over during one lesson, Hilary suggested that she take me to a meeting of Alcoholics Anonymous. I found it overwhelming to go into a church hall filled with more than fifty people. I had expected to see down-and-outs. So I was surprised to see that many of the people were smartly dressed and welcoming. A smiling lady offered me a cup of tea, and asked if I was new to the meetings. When I nodded, she gave me a hug and advised me to "listen to the similarities and not the differences when you hear the Share".

I nodded, but when I went on to listen to a confident-looking young man give the Share, describing his experience of alcoholism, all I could think was *He's not mentally ill, is he? If I didn't hear these awful voices, I wouldn't drink either.* So after the meeting was over, I ripped up the phone numbers I'd been given by the other alcoholics who wanted to help me. Then I carried on drinking.

Beth was very worried about me. We had been close friends since sixth form. She was outgoing and practical, and worked as a maths teacher in a busy comprehensive school. She had visited me some time ago in the hospital, when she had seen how withdrawn I had become as I was preoccupied with the voices. In recent months she had done her best to include me, by inviting me to parties and dinners out with her friends. One night, when she had driven us to Chelsea for some frozen ice-cream, she said, "I think you need to get out of London; why not study for a Master's at Oxford Brookes? My friend Alison has studied there, and she had a great time."

"What? I can't," I replied, feeling shocked that she had even suggested this.

"London's a bad idea for you," she replied. "If you stay here, you'll be in and out of hospital all the time, like my Uncle Nick."

I knew that her uncle had been diagnosed as 'schizophrenic'. In his early twenties he had been fired from his job as a bank cashier, as he always had the longest queues in the bank. After his diagnosis of schizophrenia, he lived with his parents until they eventually died. Nick never worked again. He had no friends, and now the only visits he got were from a psychiatric nurse, who administered a depot injection of anti-psychotic medication once a week.

"You're really quiet," Beth said.

"I know I have to change things, but I don't have the confidence to," I replied.

"Why?" she asked me.

"Well, I hear voices..." My voice trailed off.

"Is it like dreaming?" asked Beth.

"It's a bit like that," I said reluctantly.

"I have nightmares," she said encouragingly. "I wake up frightened."

A nightmare is a psychotic experience which most people can relate to, and this attempt of Beth's to put her nightmare and my voices on a spectrum with each other made me feel happier.

"I think you need to go back to what you're good at doing," said Beth. "You've always been good at studying. Why don't you give a Master's another go?"

"Do you think I could?" I asked.

"Why not?" said Beth. "It has to be better than going to the centre, doesn't it?"

I smiled at her gratefully. I realised I couldn't stand the thought of another year in that place.

Part 3
Oxford

Eleven

A month after I had moved back to Oxford, I was disappointed to find that I was still 'stuck': I was going to a Mind day-centre nearly every day to sit with other service-users. I had given up my MA in Creative Writing at Oxford Brookes University after just a fortnight, as I thought that the anti-psychotic medication had robbed me of my creativity. Often I complained about the medication to the staff at the day-centre, who would then persuade me to take it. Since the medication didn't seem to reduce the intensity or the loudness of the voices, I stopped taking it for short stretches of time, and then I would feel so anxious that I took some pills again. So, this cycle went on and on.

I liked my new studio-flat, which was in a 1960s block of flats in a leafy part of the city. It looked out on apple trees and a long lawn. I spent a lot of time on my own in the flat, reading novels or studying. Another service-user called Francesca had encouraged me to enrol with her for an AS-level course in Psychology. Francesca was a few years older than me. Tall and attractive, with large brown eyes and dark curly hair, Francesca had been a service-user for over a decade. Once a week we would travel together to a further education college in a nearby town, and I enjoyed learning about theories, such as Bowlby's theory of maternal deprivation. This theory seemed to resonate with my own life, as I could see that my mum had been distant when I was young, and that my father had abandoned me when I was still a toddler.

I was excruciatingly uncomfortable speaking up in class, and preferred to stay silent. Francesca, on the other hand, spoke far too much. She would bring up her own experiences of psychosis and electro-convulsive therapy, even when these didn't have much relevance to what the tutor was teaching us. The other students were a mixture of ages, and I saw some of them giving Francesca annoyed looks. *I'm only sitting next to her. I don't know her that well. So don't look at me as well,* I would say in my head.

Making comments in class was not the only thing I had difficulty with. I also hated using the buses, as I sometimes felt that I was being pursued by the people of my voices. This frightened me. I was also rubbish at managing my money, with my Benefits never seeming to be enough to cover my cappuccinos, make-up and the clothes that I bought to cheer myself up. My mum would have to give me hand-outs of money, and she made me feel guilty for overspending. I longed for more money and more friends, and for an identity other than being a service-user. But it didn't feel to me that working again was possible.

I was so ashamed of who I had become that I avoided visiting Granny, as I knew that I would get the 'pep talk' again of looking for work. My mum had twice visited me in Oxford, but she clearly struggled with coping with my poor mental health, and our conversations circled around taking the medication, and making more of an effort, while we ate lunch together in a restaurant that was close to my flat. Sometimes my mum would try to change the subject to a lighter topic, such as what music she was teaching her piano students, but I couldn't focus on something as 'normal' as this, and I would steer the conversation back to my mental illness. I was obsessed with thinking about my voices, which seemed louder and more intrusive than ever.

My social worker in Fulham had referred me to a GP in Oxford whom he knew. But now I was reluctant to go into the GP's consulting room for the appointment. I felt a failure since I had quit the Master's in Creative Writing. To make things worse, the voices were shouting, *She doesn't take it. She's vulnerable.* They were talking about the pills. A part of me felt paranoid. I didn't want more anti-psychotic medication. But I wanted someone to talk to, so I followed Dr Reynolds into her room. She was in her early forties, smartly dressed, with blonde curly hair and a kind face.

"It's nice to meet you. How are you?" Dr Reynolds said kindly.

"Not good," I said. "I had a breakdown recently..." My voice trailed off, and I began to sob.

Dr Reynolds handed me some tissues. I wiped my eyes as Dr Reynolds explained that my social worker in London had phoned her to let her know the situation regarding my mental health. Dr Reynolds now said, "So I suggest you come and see me once a month for a chat, and I can give you the prescriptions that you need."

I nodded, and said, "I've read that therapy can help. I'd like to see someone, even if it means paying. Is there a therapist that you can recommend?"

"Well, as it happens, there is," said Dr Reynolds, smiling. "I know a very good therapist called Daphne Coton. She's very intelligent. I send my bright patients to her. I think you'll get on with her. I'll write down her number," and she reached for a pad and a pen.

"Thank you so much," I said, taking the piece of paper and the prescriptions.

One of the mental health workers at the day-centre had found out about a 'hearing voices' training course being held at Camden Mind in London, for people who were hoping to facilitate peer support groups for voice-hearers. She suggested to me that we attend this together. I was so miserable trying to cope with the voices on my own that I agreed. The course was held on the fourth floor of a grey office block with large windows. Rai was the course facilitator - and also a voice-hearer; she was warm and chatty, in her bright red jumper and jeans.

"Could you tell the person you're sitting next to where you would visit if you could go anywhere?" asked Rai.

I froze. This was the kind of ice-breaker activity that I used to give students when I was a teacher. I didn't like being the person doing the activity.

I turned to the smiling Chinese woman next to me. "Home – Beijing," she said. "Where would you go?"

"Venice," I replied. My voice was shaking, as it was three years since I'd had a holiday. I couldn't now imagine going abroad, still hearing voices. In an aeroplane you're closed into a tiny capsule: what if I shouted back at the voices?

So I was very surprised to find out that morning that Rai had recently flown back from a mental health conference in New York. She was hearing over ten different voices, nearly all of the time. They even had names that she'd given them, like 'the Scream'. Some of the voices she hated, as they made her afraid and anxious; other voices she welcomed, as she had made friends with them. The thought of inviting in my own voices filled me with alarm. So when Rai asked people to volunteer their own lived experience that afternoon, I was reluctant to put up my hand. I didn't want to share anything about the voices, as they felt so personal to my experience.

"Yes, you can live with voices," Rai said to the group. "That's how you guys are going to help each other, as you'll be giving voice-hearers a safe space where you can talk about your voices in groups, and support each other."

My hand shot up. "Could you tell us some coping strategies for dealing with the voices? My voices are really nasty to me."

Rai smiled, and said, "I've got a hand-out with coping strategies on it. And I'm going to run through a couple of strategies that I've found really helpful, like writing down what the voices say in cartoon bubbles, and talking back to the voices."

I stared at her. I hadn't ever dared to engage with my voices by having a dialogue with them. I had only ever told them to shut up!

After the course finished, I met Daniel in a crowded coffee shop close to the Underground station. He kissed me on both cheeks. "How was the course?" he asked me.

"Really good," I replied. "Rai who ran the course is a voice-hearer, and she doesn't take medication. She doesn't seem to mind hearing her voices."

"Maybe you can learn how she copes with them," said Daniel.

"Maybe," I said in an ambivalent tone.

Daniel went to get us each a cappuccino, as I reflected on the course. When I had been discharged from the hospital, I had been told that I had a chemical imbalance in my brain, and I needed to be on medication for the rest of my life, or I'd have another breakdown. But Rai clearly coped well with her voices, and she'd told us that she didn't take medication. Earlier she'd shared that she was part of a movement of voice-hearers who accept their voices. Some even welcomed hearing them.

When Daniel returned with the cappuccinos, I said, "But isn't it strange for someone to hear voices?"

"I don't know," said Daniel. "I think I hear a voice sometimes."

"I don't think they're the kind of voices that I hear," I replied.

My voices were chattering again. I felt worried.

Were the voices spying on me? I was determined to distract myself, so I said, "So what's your voice like?"

Daniel took a sip of his cappuccino, and looked thoughtful. "When I lie in bed reading, before I put the lights out, I find my eyes will close and then I do hear a voice saying something," he said. "I realise my mind has turned into switching off mode, just as you might get a spark if you flick a switch. It's not threatening in any way. I don't know what they're saying."

"Do you recognise the voices?" I asked him.

"It might be somebody's voice I know. The voices often belong to people I've talked to during the day," he replied.

"Why do you think you hear the voices?" I said.

"It's almost as if the brain has short-circuited to a memory of some kind. It's only momentary," he replied. "It happens when sleep is overcoming me."

I decided that his voices were different from mine, as my voices sounded as if they came from outside my head. Sometimes, like now, it felt as if the men and the spiteful woman were actually there. I heard them now discussing me. This disturbed me again.

"She doesn't want her attention tricked," the man with the brittle voice was saying.

Was someone going to trick my voices, so that they were different? The thought frightened me.

"You're quiet. Are you all right?" Daniel asked me.

I nodded. I wanted to cover up the fact that I was hearing a voice, so I said quickly, "I was thinking about what you've told me about your voices. It's interesting that it happens when you fall asleep."

"That's because sleep is overcoming me," said Daniel, and he smiled.

I smiled back. I remember wishing that the voices I heard would change into the voices that Daniel experienced. His voices sounded as if they had kind tones. Maybe I could work on my relationship with my voices, so that I wasn't so scared of them? Better still, I might stop hearing voices. It was because I wanted the voices to go away that I then decided to see the therapist recommended by Dr Reynolds.

Daphne Coton's office was actually a room on the ground-floor of her home, an old, red brick Oxford house surrounded by a high wall and shrubs. Daphne herself greeted me at her front-door: she was medium height, average build, grey-haired and academic-looking, wearing glasses and a trouser-suit. She had a kind manner, and soon put me at my ease. This was helped by the fact that her wall was lined with books, including Virginia Woolf's novels. I knew that Woolf had been a voice-hearer.

"So what brings you here?" asked Daphne.

"I hear voices." I heard myself at a distance, and felt concerned by how shaky my voice sounded. "I've been told that I have schizo-affective disorder, and before that I was bipolar. The labels have just made things worse. The schizo-label makes me feel that I'm really mad."

"Does it?" asked Daphne, looking thoughtful.

"Yes," I muttered, and I felt my cheeks turn hot.

"Well, in therapy we don't use labels. Instead, we explore what's going on for you."

I was relieved to hear this, and I said, "I've

looked up schizophrenia and I don't think that my symptoms are the same as what the websites describe."

"The labels are for the convenience of the clinicians," said Daphne. "A label can't fully describe a person and how they feel."

"Do you think you can help me get rid of the voices, because I hate them," I said. In Daphne's office now, I couldn't hear the voices, and I wondered for a moment if this was because I'd started therapy.

"I can't promise that," said Daphne. "The voices are parts of yourself, so you're probably going to have to learn to live with them."

"My medication doesn't get rid of the voices," I said.

"A pill can't do that. We all hear inner voices," Daphne replied. "It's just that yours are outside your head. So you have to work hard to remind yourself that they come from within you. And that it's your mind creating them."

Daphne then went on to explain how psychotherapy would work. We would meet once a week and I would pay £50 per session. I could bring anything that was on my mind to the sessions, and share it with her. I felt happier knowing that I had somewhere to take my worries and fears.

Twelve

The next scene finds me in the dining area of Restore's Elder Stubbs project, pushing another letter into an envelope. I had thought that I would be doing useful voluntary work if I assisted the festival coordinator with the admin for a mental health festival. No, I was wrong. I hadn't spent years studying to end up doing this, feeling stressed out by the monotony of it. Why couldn't I have a proper job again that was challenging, and that paid good money? Here I was being a volunteer when I was twenty-five years old.

Daphne had encouraged me to do this volunteering, as she told me that "Restore is unique in the services it offers people who are recovering from mental health problems." Now, I thought that she was wrong. My time was being wasted. I stared bluntly at the wall. *The men were outside, surely?*

"She wants to spend time alone," the man with the brittle voice was saying.

"I definitely think she's autistic," said the neutral voice.

No, I wasn't! I was worried that I might talk back to the voices. If that happened, the staff here would think I was crazy. I just wished I was cocooned safely in my flat, reading a book. I dropped the envelope onto the table, and started to cry.

"Would you like to take a break?" said Amber, who was the support worker. Thin, tall, with curly chestnut hair, her voice was calm and soothing.

I nodded, and went over to the window to watch the other service-users gathering vegetables from the allotment for lunch. Organic fresh lunches were cooked daily on the premises by the service-users.

"She's lazy. She thinks she's too good for this," the man with the brittle voice was saying. I looked over my shoulder, but no one was there. This was my voice that I was hearing.

Amber came over and put her arm round me. "I'm sorry you're having a difficult time," she said sympathetically.

"It's just that I'm used to earning money. Now I'm only a volunteer," I said, as tears dripped down my cheeks.

"You'll work again. It'll just take time," said Amber. "Here, have some tissues," and she passed me a well-used box.

I sniffed and blew my nose. "Thanks. I'll give this a good try, and stick with it until the festival." I managed a weak smile.

Amber smiled and said, "That's good to hear. In the meantime, if you're finding things difficult, please come and talk to me. I'm here to help."

I nodded. I appreciated the fact that she hadn't tried to patronise me, as so many mental health professionals had done in the past. At least here I didn't have to pretend things were fine when they weren't. I could be myself.

I was having difficulties with low mood and the voices again, so Dr Reynolds referred me to a psychiatrist, who arranged for me to have regular meetings with a community psychiatric nurse. I didn't like Pam, who was the stout and matronly type, and spoke to me as if I was a child. She saw me as being non-compliant with medication, and kept advising me to cut down my alcohol intake, which irritated me. But it was her interference in my relationship with my mum that I found infuriating.

Pam had arranged a meeting with my mum and me in the café garden at Restore.

"I keep telling Emily that she needs to mix more," my mum said to Pam. "I'm sure that all this time she spends on her own isn't good for her."

"She's doing the volunteering at Restore," replied Pam. "I've also told Emily about a local sports and social group for people who are recovering from mental health problems. It's been set up by service-users, and I think it's a great idea."

"Are you going to go there?" Mum asked me.

"Yes," I shot back.

Mum turn to Pam, and said, "She says she'll do something, then she doesn't keep it up." Mum turned back to me, and said, "Emily, you'd feel better about things if you kept yourself busy."

How do you know? I thought, staring grimly down at the crumbs on the table. *If only they'd stop talking about me as if I wasn't here.*

Beth came to visit me on her way to a friend's party, and we drove to Blenheim Palace to have a look round. Winston Churchill had been born there over a hundred years ago, and the glass cabinets in the corridor housed his toy soldiers, arranged in neat rows. He had played with these as a child. But I liked the library best, with its gold-edged books filling the shelves, and the wonderful grand piano.

Beth saw me looking at it, and smiled. "Do you still play the piano?" she asked.

"Not now. I don't think I could. I'm out of practice," I replied.

"Do you think that Churchill played it?" asked Beth.

"He might have done. He did a lot of things," I said. We had just read about how he was a qualified bricklayer, and he did oil paintings and wrote history books for which he was awarded the Nobel Prize, all on top of being a busy politician. I now said, "Churchill was bipolar, you know. He called depression 'his black dog'."

"That's interesting," said Beth. "It shows how mental illness happens to really intelligent people who are creative. Perhaps they're more sensitive to things that don't worry people like me so much."

"Yes," I replied. I was thinking, *But Churchill wasn't schizo-affective, was he? If only I was still bipolar.* I had read somewhere that Churchill used to step back from the platform when a train was approaching, so that he wouldn't throw himself under it.

"Have you thought of joining an orchestra?" asked Beth. "You were really good at the cello, and music would be a way of meeting men."

"I might," I replied. "But it's ages since I played."

"There must be loads of orchestras in Oxford," said Beth.

"Yes, there will be," I replied. *But I wasn't feeling confident enough to join an orchestra.* It was as if I was trapped within a world of illness now.

Things were going from bad to worse. During weekly sessions with Daphne, I talked about the things I planned to do, only to change my mind about what these were. I also felt persecuted by the owners of the voices, as I believed they were spying on me. More than once, I wanted to get up and rush out of Daphne's house, and I vowed that I wouldn't come back. But Daphne kept bringing me back to the present moment, and she was careful to be gentle in the questions she asked me.

I felt enormous relief to know that I wasn't being judged by her.

Daphne was keen for us to talk about the voices. "The spiteful woman is part of you. She's the critical part," she said.

"But she feels separate," I shot back.

"Yes, I know it can seem like that. That's because the voice is outside your head."

My alcohol intake in recent weeks had doubled, as I was using drinking as a way of trying to subdue the voices, and to feel less depressed. I was so hung over in the mornings that I'd arrive late for the voluntary work at Restore. I found the admin work boring, but

I think that Amber guessed this, which was why she put me in touch with an employment specialist at Restore who could help me make applications for paid work. But I was worried about losing my Benefits, which I knew could happen if I was seen to be functioning well enough to work more than a few hours per week. Daphne called this the 'Benefits trap', and explained that the way the welfare system was structured discouraged people with mental health problems from going back to paid work, in case they couldn't sustain this, as sometimes it was difficult for them to get back on Benefits again. This was a problem that gave me an excuse to drink more wine, as my work ethic was such that I didn't feel comfortable not having a job. In fact, I worried that others would view me as being 'lazy', for I was aware of the headlines in newspapers that referred to Benefits claimants in really derogatory terms.

I didn't usually go to community activities or social events, for fear that people would ask me, "What do you do?" I felt that I couldn't lie, and I didn't have a good answer. More than once, I made up that I was finishing my Master's, but this made me feel depressed, as the prospect of studying at postgraduate level again felt entirely unrealistic. I was still keeping going with the AS-level Psychology, but I struggled with that at times. I had poor concentration, which in retrospect wasn't helped by drinking wine.

One night in March I went to meet Francesca for dinner (though I was already drunk), to discuss our homework for the Psychology course. I felt really depressed, and thought that I'd cheer us both up by buying dinner at an up-market Tapas restaurant. At the time I didn't realise that more red wine would tip me over the edge, so that I actually felt like killing myself. Francesca herself drank a lot of wine, and she liked having someone to drink with. I was slurring my words as I said, "I can't go on with things the way they are."

"Yes. Yes you can," said Francesca, and she topped up her glass with more wine.

"No, I can't. I wanted to achieve," I replied.

"Why do you have to put so many demands on yourself?" she replied. "I don't do that."

"But you don't want to get a Master's," I replied.

"No. I left Cambridge. I was in my first year of studying French when I got ill. I tried going back, but I got manic again, so I decided to leave." She looked hurt as she said this.

I was so drunk that I didn't think about Francesca's feelings in bringing up her past, and I carried on. "You're okay, your family loves you whatever you do. But in my family you have to achieve to get their respect."

"They don't sound nice," she said abruptly. "Your problem is your family. You know you don't have to buy in to what they think."

"No," I said miserably, and took another long sip of wine. I was feeling dizzy from the alcohol, but I didn't want to stop drinking.

"I've got to leave now," said Francesca. "Cheer up, Emily. It might help if you stopped putting pressure on yourself. I don't feel sorry about what I haven't achieved, do I? I accept things the way they are."

That's your problem! You don't have any ambition, I thought, as I drank more wine. After

Francesca had gone, I didn't go home, but stayed in the bar and finished the bottle of wine. It was when I was drinking that I decided to send a text to my mum telling her how I couldn't stand my life and I wanted to end it. Then I turned off my phone.

When I got back to my flat that evening, waiting outside was a police car. "Are you Emily?" asked a male police officer gently. "Your mum's called us, as she's very worried about you. We'd like to get you some help."

I nodded. "I'm all right," I said.

"We don't think you are. Let's go back to the police station for a cuppa," he replied. His hand was on my arm, and he was guiding me gently and firmly in the direction of the police car.

That night I only had a brief wait in the police station before I was taken to a hospital, where I was kept in a room that had just a bed in it that was fixed to the floor. A nurse took my handbag from me, and I was asked to remove my shoes; I was given paper slippers to wear. Next I was driven to another hospital, where I was shown to a room that had a bed with a lumpy plastic mattress. I got two hours of sleep, and felt more depressed than ever the next day.

I didn't like the other patients on the ward: they were noisy and inconsiderate. I still binged on food when I was stressed, so I made myself a pile of buttery toast in the ward's kitchen, at which point the psychiatrist came in to see me.

"Could I talk to you?" said Dr Shaw gently. She was middle-aged, but still looked youthful, with clear skin, long dark hair and hazelnut eyes. I had seen her in an outpatient's appointment some weeks before.

"I'm in the middle of a binge," I replied.

"Well, I don't have time to come back today. I'd appreciate it if I could speak to you now," she said.

I nodded, as I watched Dr Shaw sit down and open her laptop. She looked very organised.

"I hear that things reached a crisis point last night," she said. "Could you tell me about what happened?"

"I was drinking wine, and I felt really depressed," I said.

"Drinking wine can make you depressed," she replied.

I continued. "The trouble is the diagnosis. I don't want to be schizophrenic. I know I'm never going to get better."

Dr Shaw said, "I don't think it's that. I was going to say that I've read through all your medical notes. You had a difficult time in your childhood and teenage years. When there has been trauma, it can affect how your personality is formed. I think that the right diagnosis is borderline personality disorder." She paused, and then said, "I think that you'd be helped by a referral to the Complex Needs Service."

I was upset that she thought there was something wrong with my personality. "I don't need to be referred there," I said quickly. "I've already got a therapist."

"I didn't know that," replied Dr Shaw.

"She was recommended by my GP," I replied.

"Oh, that sounds good," said Dr Shaw. "If you have a therapist who you relate well to, that can really help. The type of therapy doesn't matter as much as the quality of the relationship.

I was relieved that I wouldn't have the schizo-affective label any longer, as the stigma attached to it was terrible. I began to feel that I could trust Dr Shaw. I realised that she wanted to help me.

In the end I was a voluntary patient in the hospital for three weeks. I was given a blood test to check my liver function, and I had to take Librium for the first few days after I had stopped drinking, which was a sedative. A nurse advised me to go to a meeting of Alcoholics Anonymous that happened on Sunday night in the hospital. I did go to a meeting where I heard a Share given by a smartly dressed, small-boned woman with curly grey hair and a kind face. I related to her story because she had also suffered from low self-confidence and used to drink for her emotional problems. Hannah was a special needs teacher, so I felt that she would be understanding of my difficulties. Fortunately, Hannah agreed to be my Sponsor, and suggested that we meet for coffee at her house once I was discharged from the hospital. I quickly agreed. I felt grateful that I had support from someone outside the psychiatric system, who could offer a fresh perspective.

"Remember we've all been there," said Hannah. "Alcohol doesn't solve anything, it just makes problems worse."

"Alcohol makes me feel really depressed," I replied.

"It will do," Hannah agreed. "There have been a few members of my family who've had mental difficulties. So I have some understanding of mental illness. If you're feeling like a drink, you need to do something else - like call a friend, or clean out a cupboard."

"Yes, I know," I replied.

"The compulsion to drink will go away. It's only momentary," Hannah said.

I hoped that she was right. This approach was certainly worth a try. I had learned that I didn't need to believe in God to be a member of Alcoholics Anonymous. I was desperate not to pick up another drink after I was discharged from hospital. For I now knew that I would only stay out of hospital if I didn't drink alcohol.

Thirteen

In May, I went down to Surrey to visit Granny for lunch. Daphne had encouraged me to visit Granny, as I felt guilty that I hadn't visited her for several weeks. In recent months Granny had physically declined, and living with her now was a carer in her fifties. The carer made us both a corned beef hash lunch, and popped out to the shops for a couple of hours. In spite of Granny finding it difficult to manoeuvre her 'pushy' round the coffee table and armchairs in the lounge, she was in good spirits, and pleased that I'd made the effort to visit her.

I wanted to be positive - and some things were going well. I had stopped drinking wine for two months now, and my improved concentration meant that I was doing well with the AS Psychology course. I had started playing badminton with the local service-user group that Pam had recommended to me. But there was still the issue of hearing the voices. Some months earlier, I had told Granny about my difficulty. But I didn't know whether to bring this up again.

"You're quiet," Granny said, sensing that

something was on my mind. "What's up?"

"I can't say," I replied.

"Go on. Remember that a problem shared is a problem halved," she said.

It was one of Granny's old sayings. I wasn't sure if it was true in this case, though.

"It's the voices," I said hesitantly.

"Are you hearing them now?" Granny asked me.

I nodded.

"Well, tell them to buzz off, and go back to where they come from," Granny suggested.

An image came into my mind of the voices vanishing like spectres into the corners of the room. Could that happen? There came into my mind the memory that my grandparents had had a friend called Doug who had struggled with mental illness. He had been a bomber pilot in the Second World War. So I asked Granny, "Do you remember Grandpa's friend Doug?"

"Yes, a lovely man," Granny said, and she smiled. Her mind was very sharp when it came to remembering friends from years ago.

"He used to have nightmares, didn't he?" I asked her.

"Yes, dreadful nightmares," replied Granny. "His wife used to talk about them. She got woken up too." I knew that Doug had dropped a bomb on a school in Germany, and it killed lots of children. He only found out afterwards.

"Do you think he heard voices as well?" I asked her. I had read that soldiers who had suffered complex trauma because of combat stress could often hear voices.

"I don't know if he did," Granny replied.

"Oh," I said, feeling disappointed, because I had thought of Doug as being a good example of someone who had recovered from their mental difficulty. After the war he had worked in the bank with Grandpa.

"But I do know that for a while he had awful difficulty with those nightmares of his, as did many men who fought in the war." Granny's face brightened, and she said, "They were able to overcome their difficulties, as I know you are going to, my girl."

I managed the hint of a smile. "Do you really think so?"

"I know so," she replied, and her hand reached for mine and gave it a tight squeeze

July came, and I was at the mental health festival held on Restore's allotment, helping on the bric-a-brac stall. In the last two months I had felt more positive, and I was pleased that I had helped to advertise the festival by dropping flyers through people's letterboxes. And now here I was just taking psychiatric medication for short periods when I had bad days. But mostly I had good days when I didn't need to take medication. I still went to the psychiatrist's outpatients' group, and had coffee afterwards with the other service-users. My psychiatrist and the group had encouraged me to apply for a Master's that I had found when searching on the internet - an MSc in Psychology at Oxford Brookes. I was interested in studying mental illness memoirs, and finding out more about how mental health conditions were understood by clinicians. I'd been standing at the stall for some time, and it was now quiet, so I said to Amber, "Could I have a look round the other stalls?"

"Yes, do, that's a good idea," she replied, smiling.

I wondered how popular the 'Recovery' stall was, which had been my idea. It had a felt wall with green stalks stuck on it, and the idea was that people added sunflower heads on which they wrote a phrase or word about what recovery meant to them.

It was surprising that there were so many sunflowers on the wall. I had been seriously ill recently - mental illness was real - and I had felt at times that I couldn't recover. My eyes skimmed over the sunflower heads and read: "you get told, pull yourself together", "being positive", "keeping going when the going gets tough", "having good friends", "facing stigma". Daphne had told me that I stigmatised myself. But did I experience stigma? I wondered. I resented having been given different mental health labels, and having to take pills sometimes. I also thought that others stigmatised me. Earlier in the afternoon my mum had visited the festival, while my stepdad waited outside in the car. My stepdad and I weren't on speaking terms. He probably didn't like the idea of seeing crazy people. My mum was enthusiastic about the festival, and she had liked meeting my friend Lenny, but I could tell that she wasn't comfortable standing near another elderly man who was muttering to himself. Both Lenny and I looked normal, so we didn't make people afraid of us. But what if it had been me who had been talking to my voices?

I sought comfort in retreating from the world to safe spaces, like Restore. But what was it going to be like when I started back at Brookes again? My determination to go back to university and undertake a Master's was not a small decision to undertake. I knew that it was going to come with pressures and challenges, and I was worried about whether I would cope with my voices. But I believed myself to be intelligent and driven.

It was odd being back in a seminar room. Autumn was rainy and cold, but outside the trees were still leafy. The room was full of students of a range of ages and professions. One student was in his early thirties, and worked at the charity Mind. He seemed really intelligent, and I worried if I'd be able to keep up with him.

I had no way of knowing then that a couple of the other students were also anxious about returning to studying, after a long break from university.

I didn't hear any voices that afternoon, so I relaxed. I was curious to find out more about the course. For the next couple of hours, I listened to the tutors tell us about the structure of the course, the coursework that would be involved, and other practicalities such as the libraries that we would be able to access. I hadn't studied in a university library for ages. A few months earlier, when Lenny had visited Oxford, he had encouraged me to go into the local library while he waited in a nearby café; but I'd felt stressed seeing how busy it was, and this triggered my voices. So I had left after just twenty minutes.

When at last the seminar ended, the man who worked at Mind, called David, suggested that we all go to the pub. I wanted to look sociable, and I didn't mind going to a pub and not drinking wine, so I joined the group. I didn't feel the surge of adrenalin and anxiety that I was expecting, and I found that I could make small-talk with the others about the course.

But for me, the most difficult part was the conversation that happened later in the pub. Cecily was a young clinician, with a girlish face and a head of thick chestnut hair, who was outgoing and chatty. She was taking a year's break from psychiatry. I listened as she informed David about electro-convulsive therapy. "It's a gold standard treatment in the NICE guidelines, so yes, I'd recommend using it in some cases if medication hasn't worked," she told him.

I was now interested, and said, "Have you ever administered ECT to anyone?"

"Yes. I didn't get much training to do it. I only had a couple of training sessions, and then they were wheeling a patient in," Cecily replied. "But the results were impressive. Beforehand one woman was so depressed she didn't make eye-contact and she hadn't spoken to anyone for weeks. Then, after a couple of ECT sessions, she was talking again."

"But what if a person has personality changes?" I asked. "My friend had ECT. She said that it made her less outgoing." I was thinking of Francesca, who had undergone three courses of ECT when she was in her early twenties, as her bipolar disorder had meant she had become severely depressed.

"Well, we don't know exactly how ECT works," said Cecily. "Unfortunately, personality changes can happen. But we only use ECT when we don't have any other alternative."

"My friend also said that she couldn't remember things afterwards," I said.

"Well, memory loss is one of the problems," replied Cecily, taking a long sip of her wine.

I decided that ECT wasn't worth the risks, and if I had another breakdown, I'd try anything else but that. I hoped I'd be all right now, as I was back in university, and managing to chat to people who didn't have my mental health difficulties.

Studying for the Master's meant that I began to read books about mental illness. I became really curious about my own mental health condition, and how it affected me.

But I was still very reluctant to share anything about my mental illness in the meetings of Alcoholics Anonymous. Years later, it occurs to me that I could hear a story of a drunk vomiting in the gutter, screaming insults at a policeman and even punching him, and see the person in a different light now that they had left their rock-bottom behind them. But at the time I couldn't be as forgiving of someone like myself who heard voices, as I believed that at any moment they might break down and behave in a bizarre way. In fact, what I was worried about was whether I'd have another breakdown, as my last breakdown still felt fairly recent.

I was now going to meetings of Alcoholics Anonymous three or four times a week in different church halls in central Oxford. My sponsor, Hannah, had told me that only if I attended the meetings regularly would I be able to keep off the drink.

At these meetings I started to become friendly with several people. Marcus was an actor in his late forties who had taken early retirement. He was tall, slim, with a boyish face and curly black hair. Marcus and I were often in meetings together, and a couple of times he had approached me to ask how I was finding it. Other than that, we'd never really spoken.

We first talked in the café opposite one of the meetings, one crisp bright morning when there was the delicious smell of brewing coffee. A group of six or seven of us sat round a long table in the café.

And then began one of those conversations that flowed effortlessly – Marcus and I talked about his dog Monty, and he showed me photos of a collie that was similar to the one that Grandpa had when I was a little girl. We talked about who our families were. He told me how when he was a young man he had done the washing up in the well-known café where we were having coffee. He had considered becoming a chef, because he loved cooking. I told him that I was a terrible cook, and he offered to teach me some new recipes. I didn't fancy Marcus, but I liked him a lot and felt comfortable in his presence. In fact, I felt so relaxed that I told him the truth about how I had come to be living in Oxford again. I admitted that alcohol had such a hold over me that my mental health had been terrible, and I felt that I had no choice but to return to a place where I had felt happier.

"That makes a lot of sense," said Marcus. "Alcohol can make you lose the plot."

"I know. I've heard voices," I said quickly.

"So have I. Quite a few of us have," he replied.

"So what was it like?" I asked Marcus.

"What...when I heard voices?" he said.

"Yes," I replied.

Marcus looked thoughtful, and then said, "Well, it only happened once. I was a bit drunk and I was under tremendous emotional stress."

"Go on," I said.

"Well, it was the old cliché...end of relationship... Well, in fact we were engaged." Marcus paused for a moment. "She'd been living with me, and she moved out. And it was doing my nut in, so much so that I couldn't sleep in the bed we shared, and I thought I should temporarily move into the spare room."

"Is that when you heard the voice?" I asked him quickly.

"Yes... Well, I remember I was pretty drunk that night, and I kind of collapsed into bed and turned the light out, and suddenly clear as a bell I heard her voice," Marcus replied.

"What did she say?" I said.

"She said that everything was going to be fine," said Marcus. "She was going to stay with me, and that everything could be fixed."

"Did it feel like she was actually there?" I asked him.

"Yes, it did. I turned on the light, fully expecting to see her," Marcus said.

"Were you disappointed when you didn't?' I asked him, feeling curious.

"Yeah, gutted," Marcus replied, looking disappointed. "Well, the weird thing was that even though I knew this was just a voice, I actually wished I could hear it again, even though I knew it wasn't real, if you get my drift."

I took comfort knowing that Marcus had heard

voices as well. When Marcus and I came to know each other, his jokes nearly always cheered me up. He was even good-humoured when he had the demanding job of teaching me how to cook various dishes, including Gordon Ramsay's special dish of lemon and honey chicken. I had invited round a few new friends from AA. Ever since suffering my breakdown when I was an au pair, I'd felt nervous about cooking. That night, I had forgotten to add the honey, so the lemon chicken would have tasted very acidic, if Marcus hadn't noticed this.

"Don't hold the saucepan out there," he said, as I now stirred in some spoons of honey.

"Here, give me that," Marcus said. "This is what you're doing." In a clown-like way he now impersonated me standing at an arm's distance from the saucepan. "You can't cook like that," he said, and Marcus stretched his arm out holding the saucepan, as he staggered from foot to foot clumsily, and then pretended to fall over. I laughed, for it was very funny. But after this, I still found it hard to change my ways, as part of me was frightened of burning the food. Marcus got it. The fear of cooking was in my mind.

Fourteen

I was really struggling with my first presentation for the Master's course. I had very black-and-white thinking as I sat in Daphne's office, and I now very much doubted whether I would be able to stay on the course. I pictured myself sitting in the Mind day-centre again, drinking cups of tea and moaning about medication. I didn't see any other option.

"What's the difficulty with the presentation?" Daphne asked me.

"I'm going to have to stop while I'm doing it. The voices will get too much. They'll start shouting at me, I know they will," I replied.

"You don't know that," replied Daphne. "And even if you do hear the voices, you've coped with difficult voices before."

"Not in a seminar group," I said miserably. A part of me wanted to stay on the course, so I now said, "Could I practise giving the presentation here?"

"That's fine," replied Daphne.

"I just wish that I was like the others, and I didn't

hear voices," I said.

"Well tough, you do," said Daphne. "So you've got to think of ways to cope."

I had recently spent a long time filling out a form to get a Disabled Student's Allowance for my course, which would entitle me to a new laptop. This form had been playing on my mind, and I now said, "Do you think I'm disabled?"

"You could think of it that way," replied Daphne. "But is voice-hearing any different from someone who injures their leg, and then walks afterwards with a limp? From time to time the voice-hearing might be a problem, in the same way that a physical disability is, but most of the time you manage. You live well with the voices."

I managed a smile. "I guess so," I said. "I just wish that it felt easier than it is. Sometimes I feel that I'm in a power struggle with the voices. It's them against me, and I have to win."

"A power struggle is an interesting way of looking at it," said Daphne, smiling at me.

"Well, that's what it feels like," I replied. "I only hope that I'm going to win."

I fully expected that I would have to stop during my presentation, about attachment-theory, and I had my excuse worked out. *Sorry, I'm missing a page.* It was better to make a mistake than admit to the seminar group that I was hearing voices. Scared and restless, I decided that I would remain seated at the table. I didn't want to stand up at the front, like a couple of the other students had done. I had taken a pill of Valium, knowing that it would calm me down.

I began to breathe more easily as I started to read out my paper. I took my time reading the words, and left gaps between the different sections, as a way of focusing on getting to the end. I glanced over at the others, but nobody was yawning. By the time I came to the end of the paper, I was feeling a rush of excited adrenalin.

The other students were eager to ask me questions, and the course tutor was smiling. "That was very informative and opens up some interesting points for further discussion," he said.

Thrilled, I sat back in my chair and tried to concentrate on the question that David was now asking me.

After the seminar, I went with David and Cecily to the pub and ordered a Diet Coke. I felt bitter that I couldn't celebrate my success with a glass of red wine. They were both discussing psychiatry again, and David said, "Are there any tests for mental illness?"

"No, there are no biomarkers or blood-tests that we can use," replied Cecily. "I wish there were. It would make things a lot easier."

"So, there's no concrete proof that something like schizophrenia exists?" I said quickly.

"No, not yet," said Cecily. "There's research that involves scanning the brains of schizophrenic patients. Researchers are also searching for a gene that may cause schizophrenia."

"Do you think that the illness exists?" I asked her.

"Yes, definitely," she replied. "Sometimes, when I'm working nights, I'm called to give an injection to a young guy who is really psychotic. I remember one young man who was really strong. The nurses had to hold him down while I injected him. It was quite frightening."

"It doesn't sound fun," agreed David, smiling.

I felt afraid now. I had been labelled as having psychosis. *Could I lose control like that young man? What would happen then?*

David was now telling Cecily that his girlfriend was studying to be a psychoanalyst. I wanted to get away from the topic of mental health, so I finished my Diet Coke quickly, and said, "I'm sorry, I've got to go. Tomorrow I've got a really early start." It was a lie, but I had to give some excuse for leaving early.

"Bye," they both said. Cecily continued, "See you at the course on Wednesday." A quick smile, and she turned back to David, and began chatting again.

I smiled back. A part of me felt paranoid. *Had she worked out that I'd been psychotic too? If Cecily thought I was seriously mentally ill, she wouldn't have been so easy-going and smiling, would she?*

It was chilly outside. Cars rushed past me, and I walked faster towards the bus stop. I felt so shaky that I decided to call Daniel.

"Hi, Daniel. Is now a good time to speak?" I asked him.

"Perfect. What's up?" he replied.

It felt a relief to hear his gentle, reassuring voice. I said, "I've just had a drink with people from the course. I can't work out if they know I have a mental health problem, or not."

"Why would they?" he asked me.

I said, "We were talking about psychiatry in the pub." I told Daniel the story of the young man who

Cecily had to inject with medication.

Daniel replied, "Well, they will talk about situations like that. She works in mental health, and it's part of what you're all studying."

“Yes, I guess so," I said, feeling safer that no one knew about my voice-hearing.

“Perhaps you can draw on conversations like this when you're studying mental health issues," Daniel suggested.

"Yes, that's a good idea," I replied.

I’d struggled with mental illness on my own for so long, it was a great relief to share the struggles of doing the Master’s with Daniel. This was the start of him unofficially taking on the role of being my mentor. On a bad day, when I felt paranoid, anxious and was hearing the voices, but I still had work to do, I could call him and he would help me to put things into perspective, so that I could focus on the particular task. The kindness that Daniel showed me helped me to keep going with my Master’s.

Sadly, a few weeks later I received the news that Granny’s recent forgetfulness had just been diagnosed as vascular dementia. An MRI brain scan had shown that she'd had several mini-bleeds on the brain. Her behaviour had also started to be of concern, as she was trying to cook late at night, and the fear was that she would burn the house down. This was why Aunt Janis and my mum had made the difficult decision to move Granny to a nursing home.

I found my visits to see Granny increasingly difficult, as her mental agility had gone. She would forget what I was saying, so that I had to keep repeating myself. I was very saddened by the fact that my favourite granny, who had acted as my mother, was fading away.

The therapy sessions with Daphne kept returning to how I was more resourceful than I thought I was. Daphne suggested that soft toys, nice smells like lavender and old music would be ways of connecting with Granny. My own mental health issue had made me sympathetic to Granny's illness. I decided that I would research dementia for one of my Master's essays, and I became increasingly interested in how reminiscent poetry could provide a medium for those with dementia to speak out about their experiences of living with the disease. I decided that I would try to co-facilitate poetry with Granny.

She was keen to write poems with me. I'd suggest to Granny a theme, such as going to the seaside when a child, and we explored this memory together. After that, we started the poem. If Granny had difficulty thinking of a first line, I asked leading questions: "What does your bedroom look like?" Usually, after a short time, Granny got into a flow, and I just wrote down what she said.

One afternoon, we were sitting in the garden of Granny's nursing home. It was sunny, and we had just enjoyed eating the cream eclairs that I had brought with me. Granny kept saying, "This is lovely, isn't it?"

I felt relaxed and confident that I was helping her. Granny was on such good form that we had already written two poems. I now said, "Would you like me to read out the last poem we did together?"

Granny nodded, and said, "That's a good idea."

So I started to read the poem:

My Room is My Castle

My room is my castle.
It has three solid walls,
and a fourth, with a big window.
It's very warm and comforting
and sometimes I'm alone in it
and sometimes I have friends with me.
It's a very good way of living
when you're old and getting tired,
because always the situation can fit
your present needs. It has moveable walls
and a very high ceiling
and if you wish you can reach for the stars.
With the stars come many, many memories
of a life that was young
and not so young and very old.

"Lovely, lovely," Granny said. "I'm now very old, aren't I? It's lovely to have you here, my dear."

I swallowed back my tears, as I didn't want Granny to see how upset I was. The poem had stirred up my own feelings about the recent news that her house had been sold. I'd viewed her house as my 'home', and now her world had shrunk to this small room in a nursing home. But even so, she had still managed to make it feel homely, with her stuffed animals, her paintings and the cards that I'd sent her.

The voices were chattering again. "It's her gran. She feels lonely." They were talking about me. *Just go away!* I thought. Not only was there my sadness to cope with, but, as always at difficult times, there were my voices to contend with as well.

In the period leading up to my Master's I had managed to lose a couple of stone, as I took medication sparingly and I watched what I ate like l hawk. My regained confidence in my slim body meant that I was keen to go to bed with Daniel again, as sex with him was pleasurable and uncomplicated. We both knew that it was sex with no strings attached to it. I knew that Daniel slept with other women, and I put this out of my mind.

My difficulty was that even sex stirred up a fear of intimacy, and I worried whether the voices would be difficult. Sometimes they were. I knew that I could talk to Daniel about the voices, and he didn't get freaked out. He didn't seem to stigmatise me at all. On a few occasions in the bath, where I felt safe, I even ventured to tell him more about the voices, in terms of what they said, and who they represented to me in my mind.

"It's your unconscious mind reflecting your fears," said Daniel. "Your relationship with your mother has always been difficult. Maybe the female voice represents her?"

I didn't like this thought. "Do you think so?" I said. "It doesn't sound like her."

"Well, you say that it's a voice that criticises you," he replied.

"Yes, it does. It never says anything positive." I sank down further into the warm bubbles. Resting on Daniel's chest, it felt safe to be talking about the voices.

"When the voices pick on you, why don't you question them, and say, why are you telling me this?"

Daniel suggested.

"Yes, I'll try that," I replied. "At the moment I tell them to fuck off." Nowadays, I always did this in my head, but never out loud.

"Well, they're parts of yourself," Daniel replied. "It's not nice telling parts of yourself to get lost, is it? You might find it works better to come to some understanding with them."

I now remembered that Daphne had advised that if I was hearing difficult voices, one strategy was to invite them into the room. I wondered if I should try this strategy.

That night, we were both woken by a loud noise outside in the street. I felt Daniel putting his arm gently round me, and he said, "Don't worry. It's someone outside in the street who's shouting. I didn't want you to think it was your voices."

"Thanks. I appreciate you telling me," I replied. I snuggled down further into the warm bed. I felt grateful for having Daniel there with me. I felt less alone with my voices.

My problem with intimacy was something that Daphne raised in the next therapy session, after I told her that I feared that Daniel might lose interest in me. She said, "I don't think that's likely. He's been in your life as a friend for several years." She paused, and looked thoughtful. "Your father disappeared out of your life when you were very young, and your stepfather neglected you and was occasionally violent." She left a short pause. "You had the loving relationship with your grandfather, but he died when you were only twenty. I think you worry about men abandoning you, so you don't let yourself trust them."

I felt very uncomfortable facing these facts. I found it disturbing to think that I couldn't trust men. "Do you think I can change?" I asked her.

"Talking about the issue helps. By reflecting on how you relate to men, you can begin to notice a pattern," Daphne replied.

"I know that I have difficulties with trust, but I still wouldn't like to be like my mum who is co-dependent on men," I said. "Granny used to say that Mum could never be without a man."

"Well, it sounds as if there is something in your mother which draws her to men who are unpleasant," Daphne replied.

I had previously told Daphne what I knew of my parents' divorce, which was that my mum had left my father when I was two and my brother was just six weeks old; the reason given was that he had turned up a radio very loud next to my baby brother, and my mum had feared for our safety. In fact my father was also drinking heavily and had been fired from his job as an accountant. He was being very controlling and emotionally abusive to my mum, so much so that she had to time her escape for when he was out at the shops. She had my grandparents waiting in a car down the road to rescue us.

After the therapy session was over, I was still worried. *What if I can never change? Will I always keep a man at a distance?*

I interspersed the study for my Master's with going to meetings of Alcoholics Anonymous, and sometimes meeting friends for coffee. Francesca and I used to have long picnic lunches in the park, and I would meet Marcus for ice-cream at a nearby shop. Marcus showed a real interest in my Master's, particularly the fact that I was drawn to studying voice-hearing. He praised me for being "able to get a grant out of a stone". I'd found that I was good at applying for grant money. I liked the fact that Marcus had confidence in me. It showed me that Daniel wasn't the only man who believed in my academic skills and potential.

Despite my latest diagnosis of borderline personality disorder, I still saw myself as struggling with schizophrenia. After all, I heard voices that seemed to come from outside my head, which at times made it hard to concentrate and to pretend that things were normal.

So the following summer I decided to explore this issue further as part of my research for the Master's dissertation. Relatively few memoirs were published on schizophrenia, as opposed to more common mental disorders such as anxiety or depression. It was not difficult to see why most voice-hearers chose to keep quiet about their voices, when the risk of discrimination was so great. In the introduction to my dissertation, I wrote that this would 'explore the effectiveness of the memoir form in enabling the patient with schizophrenia or schizo-affective disorder to reveal and structure what it is like to live with such an illness'. I found that in schizophrenia it is not a splitting of the individual which occurs, but a splitting of feelings and thought processes. As Elyn Saks, a professor of law and psychiatry, and a person diagnosed with schizophrenia, states: 'the schizophrenic mind is not split, but shattered'.[1] I only had to think of how I'd felt when I had my breakdown to know that this was true. Despite the possibility of stigma, Saks claimed in her memoir that it can be therapeutic to tell others about the experience of living with schizophrenia; she recommends, nevertheless, that a sufferer be cautious, balancing 'the urge to tell' with what she calls 'the inevitable consequences of telling'.[2]

I felt that I couldn't risk telling the other students on my course that I had first-hand experience of voice-hearing, and this had informed the subject that I had chosen for my dissertation. However, I did tell the tutor who ran the Master's the truth about myself. Martin was a psychologist, and I wanted to have his help with the dissertation.

Martin looked at me in a knowing way, and said kindly, "The understanding of voice-hearing has changed. It's now thought that people can live with some level of hearing voices. Before, voice-hearing was medicated with the aim of eradicating the voices."

"I know that you can live with voices," I replied. "I met a voice-hearer who likes her voices, who was the trainer on this course that I went to." I was thinking of Rai, and I continued, "She was teaching us ways that we could facilitate support groups for voice-hearers."

"That sounds interesting," Martin replied. "I know a researcher in Oxford called Hilary, who has

---

[1] Elyn Saks, *The Centre Cannot Hold: a memoir of my schizophrenia* (Hachette, 2007), p. 303.
[2] Saks, p. 267.

funding to conduct a project about voice-hearing."

I smiled.

Martin said, "Hilary might have some work for you. Would you be interested in meeting her?"

"Yes, I said quickly, for I was really keen to find paid work."

Fifteen

I was convinced that I'd only scraped a pass in my Master's, so I didn't check my result for several weeks. When finally Daniel persuaded me to go to the online portal to see my result, I was shocked to discover that I had passed the Master's with Merit. I was thrilled to have this result.

I was very grateful to Daniel for his encouragement and support during the Master's, and we celebrated by having dinner at my favourite Italian restaurant in Oxford, and enjoying passionate sex afterwards.

Then I emailed Martin's contact Hilary to arrange to meet for coffee. Beth was very encouraging, as she thought that it was good that I would be researching a practical topic. For there was more funding in subjects where it was thought there would be an outcome that could benefit the community in some way.

I felt really nervous as I walked along the street to Starbucks, where I had arranged to meet Hilary. By the time I got there, I was hearing voices, so I was surprised when the man with the neutral voice said, "It might be a good idea." *Was he talking about the job?* I wondered.

When I met with Hilary, I immediately liked her easy-going, open manner. We introduced ourselves and she asked me about my Master's dissertation. Then she told me about her research project, which would involve interviews with twelve voice-hearers. The aim of the project was to explore the kind and quality of relationship that participants have with their voices. I finally said what was on my mind: "I've had some experience of voice-hearing," I said nervously. "In fact, I've lived with mental health issues for years, but I think that this perspective will inform my research."

Hilary smiled kindly, and said, "First-hand experience is an asset in this kind of research. Several of our researchers have some kind of lived experience of different mental health issues." She smiled, and said, "This is a very good time for someone with lived experience to work in mental health research. We also offer some training in research methods."

I realised how competitive it was to get a research job. I felt that I could trust Hilary, so I suggested, "I'd like to share with the people I interview that I've heard voices, as I think that then people will trust giving me their data."

"That sounds like a very good idea," said Hilary, looking pleased.

I was confident that the interview had gone well. But the wait afterwards seemed to last forever. Then, just before 5 p.m. that day, there was an email from Hilary to say that I had got the job, and that she would be emailing me a contract.

Accepting the job was one of the best decisions I ever made. The job also involved me becoming a member of a research team. With my Master's in psychology and my lived experience of voice-hearing, I was well placed to contribute to discussions in team meetings.

But I was very nervous when I joined the team for my first research meeting with them. The meetings took place fortnightly. I was expected to attend all of them, and to go for a drink in the pub with the team afterwards. To my knowledge, I was the only member of the research team who had shared that they had experienced voice-hearing. I worried that if I mentioned that I was a voice-hearer, this would shape how they saw me in a negative way.

The meetings took place in a seminar room in the Institute of Mental Health Studies, which had a view over a leafy park. It helped immensely that the other researchers were friendly and chatty. I'd joined a group of three researchers to help plan a task that could be given to a voice-hearer when they were inside an MRI scanner, having their brain scanned.

"I've heard voices, and it can be worse if you're trapped in a tight space," I said. I was thinking about the time I had been on the Tube going into central London. "So you need to think of an exercise that doesn't put stress on them. What about playing them two or three songs to see how they react to the music?"

"That's a good idea," said a researcher who was a psychologist. "We could look at whether music interrupts their voice-hearing. There are some studies to show that music can do this."

"What music would you play?" asked a professor.

"What about a David Bowie song?" suggested the psychologist.

I liked the fact that the academic hierarchy that existed between us didn't seem to be there as we all focused on how this study with the voice-hearer might work.

As the meetings went by, my confidence grew somewhat, and it became easier for me to make comments in the discussions. The research project also gave me opportunities to get involved in other ways, and I wrote a short story about my experience of hearing voices, which I read out loud at a mental health conference.

During these months, I had an office that I shared with two psychologists, and I enjoyed working there. I still regularly had appointments with Daphne. Knowing that I had this support from Daphne made all the difference, as I was able to talk about the stresses I faced, such as the long hours of work I needed to do, and Granny's dementia.

I continued to attend AA meetings, and I remained sober. I could also get down to Surrey fairly easily to visit Granny and my mum, and I carried on finding ways to connect with Granny, such as writing the poems. Mum still paid for my therapy. She wanted the job to be a success, as she could see how hard I was trying. She insisted that I show her my bank statements when we meet, as she was helping me financially. My mum taught me how to be careful with money, and she helped me to clear my debts, so that I am now in a good position financially.

I was shocked one evening to receive a call from Mum to say that Granny had fallen and broken her hip, and would need an operation to have her hip pinned. She survived the operation, and the following Saturday I went to visit her in the same hospital where Grandpa had died. I felt really distressed when I pulled back the curtain and found her sat on a commode. Granny was crying, as she needed help to stand up. The ward was massively understaffed, as it had only opened in winter to take the growing number of elderly people who needed care.

My distress that day then increased. My brother Dan had timed his visit to the ward to coincide with my own. Apart from family Christmases, we hadn't had anything to do with each other for years. Following the difficulty of my anorexia when I was a teenager, he had developed ME, an illness which meant that he became exhausted all the time. My mum had been unable to cope with the situation, so he had spent increasing amounts of time at my grandparents' house, sleeping in one of their spare bedrooms until he was living there temporarily. In the end, he did recover to the point where he was able to study for his A-levels over three years. He'd gone on to read Psychology at university, but he carried with him the resentment that the distress created by my anorexia had caused his ME. We'd grown so far apart that he hadn't invited me to his wedding, and my mum hadn't told me about it until months later.

I found my brother manipulative, and it seemed to me that he always wanted to control the situation so that he got a favourable outcome. That afternoon was no exception. We talked about Granny for a while, and I asked after my brother's baby daughter and his business. Ben suddenly said, "I don't know if Mum's told you, but I've managed to trace our dad. It's been something I've wanted to do for a long while. Then I decided that if I left it any longer, it wasn't going to happen."

I felt as if I'd been punched in the stomach. "What? I thought he was dead," I blurted out. There had been no mention of my father for so many years that I'd assumed that he had drunk himself to death years ago.

"In the end it was quite easy to trace him," Ben said. "I looked up his name in the phone directory, and found that there was a Saul N. living in Brighton."

"Is he still alive?" I gasped.

"Yes. He had a heart bypass a couple of years ago. But he's made a good recovery," Ben replied. "He'd like to meet you, but he understands that it's up to you to decide. He's very remorseful that he hasn't been in contact for all these years. He said that he wanted to get in touch with us long ago, but after the divorce he felt that he couldn't."

"I see," I replied, feeling giddy with anxiety.

I nearly made the decision never to meet my father. However, I received an email from him, in which he reflected on how he'd been listening to Brahms Requiem, and crying, because he thought that I didn't want to see him again. This made me think that maybe I should meet him.

We arranged to meet outside the Ashmolean Museum in Oxford on Saturday morning at 11 o'clock. I'd be wearing a black coat and carrying a red handbag, so that he'd recognise me. He also had my mobile number, in case his train was delayed.

Daniel had told me to have 'no expectations', so that I didn't get disappointed. He also advised me not to take my father back to my flat, saying "You are, after all, meeting a stranger, although of course it's your dad." I listened to Daniel; I knew exactly what he was talking about. My father wasn't to be trusted. I knew that my mum was very worried about this meeting, as she didn't want "my father causing me a setback after all of the effort that I'd put into my recovery".

Despite my apprehension, I also felt tremendously excited at meeting my father. In our next therapy session, Daphne said that this mixture of emotions was normal, as I'd wanted a father so much when I was growing up. I had no conscious memory of him. Now, at the age of twenty-six, I was very curious to meet the man from whose genes I had been created. Saul, my father, had sent me photos of himself, and while we didn't look alike, I did have his dark hair and bushy eyebrows. I disliked my eyebrows, and spent money on having them threaded.

The man who walked up the stone steps towards the museum didn't look like my father in the photos. He looked very fat in his green parka, and he had an overly self-confident smile that made me nervous. He said, "It's you. It's little Emily." Then, he was wiping tears from his eyes.

With intense effort, I held back my tears.

Up close I saw that he had broader features than me. His eyes were a different colour – they were brown, and his nose was larger than mine. My face bore a strong resemblance to Granny's face in photos taken of her when she was young.

He took my hand in his, and put his arm around me. Then his hand stroked my face, and he kissed my cheek. I felt uncomfortable with how tactile he was being.

"Shall we go around the museum?" I said quickly. I thought that it would help us to have a focus.

As we went round, I certainly couldn't focus on the Roman statues and mummies. *Yes, yes, it was really happening – I was here with my dad.* "I blame your grandmother for this not happening before," said Saul suddenly.

"What?" I said.

"Your grandmother stopped me from seeing you when you were very small. I should have stood up to her," he said. "When I used to visit you, after your mum had left me, Vera kept interfering. She did it deliberately. She drove me away." Saul had started to cry again, and I watched as he wiped his eyes. He said, "Sorry, it's just that I wish I'd come back and seen you before." He reached his hand out and stroked my face again.

I felt very upset that Saul was blaming Granny for the fact that he'd not seen me before. In fact, it was Granny who had encouraged me to meet him all these years later. In the nursing home, she had told me that "my father was a warm man". Granny could remember the past and she had also added that she had no father herself from the time she was four years old, as her parents divorced. So she thought that "it was good to have this reunion". But, when I repeated this to Mum, she said, "Granny doesn't know what she's saying, so don't listen to her." Now, I didn't know what to think.

I had planned to take my father for lunch at a pleasant, cheap café round the corner. I knew that he lived in a council bungalow and that he didn't have much money. I imagined that he'd want to buy lunch for both of us. He was pleased with the full English breakfast that he ordered for himself. I was eating a tuna mayonnaise jacket potato, as I was watching my weight as usual.

Some way into lunch, Saul said, "I wasn't always skint. I got done by the police for fraud a few years back, so my accountancy firm went bust."

There was an awkward pause, as this news sank in. "I'm sorry," I said, for I couldn't think what else to say.

Saul continued: "The court ordered me to work a hundred hours in a charity shop afterwards." His self-confident smile was back, and he said, "I got together with one of the volunteers there for a fling, so it wasn't much of a punishment!" He laughed.

I felt shocked to hear this. I hadn't imagined that my father would be on the wrong side of the law. My grandparents and my mum had always been so honest about money. I'd been brought up not to cheat people.

"You don't seem to care much about money," said Saul. "You're the academic type. You're clever, so your head is always stuck in books."

I smiled to be polite, but inside I was thinking, *Actually I do care about money.*

That meeting was to be the last I ever had with

my father. Sadly, as the day went on, it became clear to me that he was a cunning manipulator, and that he wouldn't take any responsibility for the fact that he hadn't seen me for twenty-four years. He wanted to blame my grandparents, when in fact they had been loving surrogate parents to me in his absence. I never expressed how I felt to my father. I didn't feel able to. It was as if I was acting all afternoon, as I wanted to please him. I didn't even complain when he kept trying to stroke my face, and put his arm round me, even though I hated this. I didn't hear any voices that afternoon, as I was so dissociated. It was only afterwards that every fibre of me screamed *I never want to see that man again!* It was a tremendous disappointment to me that this was my father.

Sixteen

My friends were very kind to me when I told them that the meeting with my father had been a disaster. I worked even harder at my job to try to shut out my disappointment and my anger that my father had not been a different kind of man.

Around this time Daphne encouraged me to re-establish my connection with music, as she said that it would be a helpful way of releasing my emotions. After the distress of meeting my father, I was keen to find such things to do. So I decided to get lessons with a professional cellist. Olivia taught from an office in her house. She had been a professional for many years, and regularly performed in concerts and with her string quartet. I could tell that she loved teaching, and she made the lessons unpressurised and fun. In one lesson I was playing a slow, very expressive piece by Schumann called 'Lento'. I felt close to tears when I came to the end of it.

"Didn't Schumann die quite young?" I asked Olivia.

"Yes, he didn't go on for long," replied Olivia. "He was an interesting character. He was in and out of mental hospitals. But he was still very productive. Besides composing, he wanted to be a concert pianist. So he built himself a contraption with a string from the ceiling and a special harness to strengthen the little finger on his right hand. But he ended up damaging his finger, so his dream of being a concert pianist was shattered."

"Oh no," I replied. Building the harness sounded obsessive. I wondered if Schumann had been obsessive in the same way that I was. *Did he hear voices? Was that why he ended up in psychiatric hospitals?*

I was pleased that, despite hearing voices, sometimes in my lessons I was managing to play quite complex music, and enjoying it.

My job was involving challenging research, as it required twelve interviews with voice-hearers. Sometimes I was reluctant to tell service-users in the mental health centre that I was a voice-hearer, as I wanted to keep a sense of distance between us. It was not always easy for me to remember that I was attending the mental health centres as a researcher, and not as a service-user. That said, for the most part I enjoyed the interactions I had with the service-users, as this involved lively conversations and writing field notes afterwards. For obvious reasons, I'd become interested in what it meant to have a relationship to voices, whether these are experienced as negative and overwhelming, and/or positive and creative. With the exception of Francesca, I'd stopped hanging round with other service-users from the psychiatrist's support group. I just didn't have enough in common with them to meet them for coffee. My dogged determination to get on wasn't welcomed by a couple of the members of the group. But I was prepared for this, as my GP, Dr Reynolds, had already told me that "service-users stick together, and they sometimes don't like it when someone gets better".

I motivated myself by reading memoirs of voice-hearers who had recoveries, and I took myself to inspiring mental health conferences, where people with lived experience spoke. I was on a mission. Although it was sometimes a lonely journey to being well, I drew support from my conversations with Daphne, Beth and Daniel, who were delighted that I was managing the pressures of a full-time job.

I also made some new friends through my interest in promoting mental health. I met Angela at a mental health conference in London. Angela was running the Time to Change stall, and we got talking. She was also in her thirties. Bright and outgoing, Angela managed the area from Northumberland down to Sheffield for Time to Change, a charity that challenges the stigma surrounding mental illness. I told Angela about my research.

"We don't get many volunteers who are willing to talk about voice-hearing," Angela said. "There's still a lot of stigma associated with voices."

"I know," I replied. "Actually I'm a voice-hearer. I didn't talk about my voices for years. I feared how people would react."

"Well, it's really good that you're doing it now."

"Thanks," I replied. "It's not easy. There was a

really nosy man I met recently who asked me if I liked the voices that I heard. It was none of his business."

"Some people have a voyeuristic interest, that's all. It's good that you know your own boundaries as to what you're happy and not happy to share," Angela replied.

I smiled. "It's been a steep learning curve. Sometimes now I even worry that I've shared too much. I think I'm more comfortable with doing the research than talking about my voices. I'm not even sure if I like calling myself a voice-hearer. The trouble is that if you say you hear voices, everyone thinks that you have schizophrenia when, in fact, you can hear voices with different diagnoses." I replied. "I wish the public knew that."

"Yes, I know," replied Angela.

"Well, I wish the public did," I said.

"That's why it's good what your research team are doing to educate people," Angela replied.

This was the start of several meetings with Angela for coffee, when we'd discuss the minefield of stigma which exists towards people who hear voices. I liked Angela's directness and honesty, and the way that she really cared about marginalised people with mental health issues. She didn't write people off, and she always had a good word to say about everybody.

These conversations gave me the confidence to take part in a Voice Walk at a mental health festival in London. There were five voice-hearers who gave talks about the course during this walk. My talk addressed stigma and voice-hearing, so it was fitting that opposite me was a building that was formerly St Clement's mental hospital. I could see the doorway to the hospital through which they used to carry the bodies to bury them in the cemetery. I read part of my short story about hearing voices, and then I spoke for five minutes about my recovery journey, before taking questions from the people who had come on the walk.

It was an inspiring experience to be walking with other voice-hearers, who were carrying banners that had printed on them strong messages such as "We hear voices. Listen to us." It felt as if we were challenging stigma together, and that this was, in fact, a civil rights issue, given the marginalisation, isolation and powerlessness that voice-hearers have historically experienced. The second speaker, Jeff, spoke of how psychological therapies are less likely to be offered to black and minority ethnic voice-hearers. Sam, the third speaker, described himself as a '24/7 voice-hearer', and said that he wanted to combat stigma and speak for voice-hearers who are less able to challenge prejudice. Finally, there was a co-presentation by Miranda, who had unusual experiences as a teenager, and Rai, who was the trainer who had run the course that I attended in London four years earlier. Miranda thought that it was very important for a young person to share their unusual experiences with someone they trusted. Whereas Rai stressed that despite now hearing up to thirteen voices, the voices are parts of her, and she would choose to live with them. Rai now worked creatively with young people who were voice-hearers, and encouraged them not to be afraid of their voices.

The people participating in the walk asked all five of us voice-hearers interesting questions. There were also informal conversations as we walked together, and people said that they had learned more about voice-hearing. Some people said that their ideas about voice-hearing had changed in a positive way.

For four years I hadn't had a holiday. Now, my research team was funding me to attend the 6th World Hearing Voices Congress, taking place in the culturally diverse city of Thessaloniki in Greece. Given the current economic crisis in Greece, it was highly relevant that the theme of the Congress explored 'struggling towards recovery in times of crisis'. I was hoping that the Congress would give me the opportunity to speak to voice-hearers and mental health professionals who currently facilitate hearing voices groups, and to learn from them strategies for running a helpful group for people who have unusual experiences in Oxford.

The flight was much more comfortable than I expected, as my seat was near another PhD student, and we chatted on the plane. Now at the conference, I was given a headset so that I could hear a translated version of each presentation. It was exciting to think that it was an international conference, with voice-hearers from many different countries sharing stories of their voices. The next talk was to be given by Professor Marius Romme, a psychiatrist from the Netherlands, now in his eighties, who was one of the founders of the Hearing Voices Movement. The title of Romme's speech was 'How to solve the schizophrenia problem'. The room was so full that I was forced to sit at the back. It was very warm, and I fanned myself with the programme.

For the next hour I listened as Romme argued

that there was a lack of empirical scientific evidence for the diagnosis of schizophrenia. "With schizophrenia, the symptoms are used to construct the illness," he said. "And at present, there are no biomarkers or tests for determining this." It was what Cecily had told me during my Master's.

Romme explained that 4 per cent of the general population have had a voice-hearing experience. "The illness concept discriminates against millions of people who hear voices, because generally it is seen as a symptom of an illness," said Romme. He pointed out that there are links between the characteristics of voices and the problems that a voice-hearer has faced in their past.

But many people who hear voices have never experienced a specific trauma, I thought to myself. *Voice-hearing is not just about trauma!* I thought how my own long-term neglect wasn't a specific trauma. This trauma paradigm risked being as reductive a model as the biomedical explanation that psychiatry gave for voice-hearing. I now didn't know what to think.

It was beautiful in Thessaloniki, and it was wonderful to explore the city. The Aegean Ocean was a deep indigo blue, and in the late afternoons I spent time walking along the seafront on my own, enjoying the peace after the intensity of the conference. With the heat of the sun, it was still warm in September. Astonished at my confidence in a new country, I read a map and met other voice-hearers at local cafés. I enjoyed drinking cappuccinos with cinnamon sprinkled on the top, and chatting about voice-hearing and sharing coping strategies. I met Rai, the trainer, again, who told me that she was "proud to be a voice-hearer". She was there with her husband, who seemed to be very supportive of her vocation to encourage people to live well with their voices.

But at the same time I felt lonely when I was surrounded by voice-hearers, because I knew that I didn't fully accept all the ideas of the Hearing Voices Movement. I wanted to stay in work, and I felt I needed to be discreet about voice-hearing and only disclose this to people I could trust. Some of the voice-hearers that I met in Greece didn't think there was any need for caution, but then many of them were unemployed and marginalised. I was scared of being in that position again.

Seventeen

My fear of ending up again on Benefits hadn't happened. Yet I still carried it with me. Daphne looked at me, and said calmly, "I don't think you are a service-user any more."

"But that's what I call myself when I do my research," I replied.

The expression on Daphne's face made it clear that she wasn't going to let the subject drop. She said, "Does a service-user mean someone who takes some pills sometimes, and goes to see a doctor once in a while, and receives ongoing therapeutic support?"

I knew that she was referring to me, and I stayed silent.

Daphne continued. "They might say to their doctor once in a while that some mental issue has come up for them, but that's not the same thing as having a mental breakdown."

"But I still hear voices most days," I replied.

"You can hear voices and not be psychotic. We both know that," Daphne replied.

Since I had struggled with the 'psychosis' diagnosis, I took comfort now in knowing that I could hear voices and not be 'ill'. I would often hear voices when I was stressed or tired. In fact, sometimes challenging emotions - guilt, shame or fear - led to me hearing voices, and I had recently found that the voices reduced if I expressed how I felt. This was why playing the cello was so helpful.

"But if I'm not a service-user, what do I call myself?" I asked Daphne.

"What do you think would be a good way to describe yourself?" she asked me.

I shrugged, and replied, "Maybe a researcher with lived experience." I'd heard other researchers use this title when they had experienced voice-hearing.

"That sounds fine," replied Daphne.

After the session, I turned over in my mind what had been said. I used to be so scared that I would remain stuck in the mental health system. Now I had been discharged by my psychiatrist, and I just saw my GP, Dr Reynolds, once a month for a chat and to collect prescriptions if I needed them. I could see that I was a researcher now. More than that, my experience of hearing voices was helping me to have a career. In fact, it was an advantage in this kind of research to know what it was like to hear voices.

It was for this reason that a professor from the University of Nevada, Las Vegas, who had teamed up with the research team, asked me to record my inner experience for a study that he was doing. Russ gave me a beeper, and I was to write down what I had been thinking the moment before I heard the beeper go off. If I was hearing a voice, I was to record this. Then, once I had listened to six beeps, I was to have an interview with Russ and one of the psychologists from my research team, when they would ask me questions about my inner mental experience just before I had heard these beeps. I found this process challenging, as an entry from my Reflective Journal shows:

Entry in my diary on 5 October

> *I'm glad that I've taken part in Russ's 'hearing voices' study, as it has made me think about the connection between my thoughts and what voices I hear. They do appear to be linked in thematic content. I found it difficult to talk about how the voices have physical presences, which are external to me, as if they are people. This, of course, is a delusion, so it needs to be deconstructed, which then makes it an 'illusion'.*

The opportunity to reflect on what was happening for me when the buzzer went off enabled me to start to understand my voices more. What had been for me a bewildering, frightening phenomenon was now becoming fascinating on an intellectual level. I was gaining more insight as I stepped back from the experience to examine it.

In fact, some of the myths that made voice-hearing taboo in society started to dissolve. My voices didn't tell me to kill people, and they weren't commanding. However, the voices could be manipulative, and say things that were untrue. This was when I chose to ignore the voices, or challenge them in some way. Through the course of my research, I had come to understand that my voices functioned as an internal saboteur, and made negative, critical comments about me. The voices were repetitive. When I was a child I suffered from obsessive-compulsive disorder, and even now I can have health anxiety about the pain in my back. This anxiety is obsessive, just as my voices are obsessive.

My friend Francesca couldn't understand why I kept wanting to listen to what the voices had to say. "Just tell your voices to shut up!" she said.

"They often won't go away," I replied. "That's not just the case with me. Nearly every one of the thirty voice-hearers I interviewed still hear voices. And lots of them are on medication."

Francesca sighed. "That sucks. I'm glad I'm not a voice-hearer. Depression is bad enough."

I had other focuses as well, besides exploring voice-hearing. I was now spending time playing the cello in a local amateur orchestra, and I was enjoying going on walks with a local Singles group. I was no longer sleeping with Daniel, as I wanted to find someone who wanted a committed relationship. We have remained really good friends, though, and I find Daniel very supportive, particularly when it comes to my research. But I was still lonely, and was looking to expand my social network.

I didn't want to go into the nursing home. I sensed that it would be the last time, and I didn't want to cry. In my mum's eyes, crying would make things worse. We had to be strong because Granny didn't have long. I felt terribly conflicted. In my mind it was Granny who had been my mother-figure ever since I could remember. With my own mother, it was more a performance of the roles that we were supposed to have as mother and daughter.

So I did my best to dissociate myself from my

distress. After we entered the nursing home, I calmly signed my mum's and my name in the visitors' book. Then I followed my mum down the corridor, through the little lounge where I had sat with Granny so many times doing puppet shows for her, and down another corridor to her bedroom. There she lay on her bed, turned to the wall, making whimpering sounds as if she was very frightened.

"What's wrong, Granny?" I asked her, feeling very worried.

She didn't reply, so I tried to hold her hand, which felt warm.

"Get off!" she cried out, jerking her hand back.

I felt a sharp twinge of pain inside me, as I took this to be rejection. I glanced over at my mum, who stood awkwardly beside the bed as if she didn't know what to do. I had to steel myself again, because I knew that Granny was very confused from her dementia. I thought about the times when I had heard voices picking away at me, and I had been afraid. It usually helped me to talk to a friend. So I drew a chair over to her bedside, and said, "What's happened?"

"The nurses have beaten me up," she said, and began to cry.

Granny was clearly terrified. I felt surprised to hear this. This was a dramatic shift from Granny believing that she was in charge of the nursing home. Now, she had shrunk to a tiny frail lady in her large white bed.

I now remembered that I had brought the CD player with some music to play. "I've got something for you," I mumbled. I went over to the corner of the room and plugged in the CD player; I put on the

Vera Lynn CD that the man who worked in the music shop had said was very popular with Granny's generation during the war effort. I thought that Granny would enjoy listening to a singer with the same name.

Vera Lynn's warm, plummy voice filled the room, singing "We'll meet again, don't know where, don't know when", and I noticed that Granny started to move her toes in time to the music. My mum saw this too. "Mum, you're wriggling your toes. You like this, don't you?"

"Yes, it's lovely," Granny said.

It was as if the fear of just a few moments before had fallen away, and the music brought a peace that words alone could not. I don't know how long the three of us sat still, listening to the music, but it was for quite a while. At one point Granny turned to me, and said, "Thank you for helping me." In those few moments she was fully present.

I turned to her, and said, "And thank you for everything that you did to help me when I was younger." At this point Granny smiled, and I knew that we had a mutual respect for each other.

Back in Oxford, coping with my stirred up feelings was very difficult. I felt restless, and I couldn't settle on any work. My flat felt suffocating, so I decided to go out for dinner. Outside it was freezing.

Halfway down the road the brittle male voice said, "She's going to die. That's what I think."

"It's obvious, I'm afraid," said the neutral male voice.

A chilling sensation spread through me as I

started to wonder again if these men were really there. I didn't like the idea of these men discussing Granny in this way.

I crossed to the other side of the street, and watched the shadows of branches surging in the wind. I wanted to shut out the voices. They were quieter now, like murmurs. But I still felt afraid. So I rang Daniel, and told him about my earlier visit to see Granny, and about what the voices were saying.

"Well, your grandmother probably is going to die soon," Daniel said. "Maybe you think that too, and the voices are just telling you that." His tone was kind and gentle.

"I'm sure you're right," I said. "It's just that she's suffering so much. And when she goes, I'll be on my own." Daniel knew that I had always looked to Granny as my mother-figure.

Daniel said, "But you have to remember that she's had a very long and happy life. You can't ask for more."

I felt comforted by Daniel's words, and after our phone call finished, I decided to eat an Indian curry to distract myself from how I felt.

It was a couple of mornings later that I received the call from my mum early in the morning to say that Granny had peacefully passed away just before midnight. She was with her favourite nurse when she died. Mum told me that she went to the nursing home shortly afterwards, and sat with Granny's body while she was still warm, and said goodbye. I realised that I had said goodbye in my own way when I'd played her Vera Lynn's music.

Very fortunately that morning was scheduled for my monthly routine appointment with Dr Reynolds. Sitting in the waiting room, I feared that I might start to hear the voice of my now dead grandmother. When I heard the voices they were often unkind and critical of me, so I feared this happening.

I strained to listen for the voices, but I couldn't hear anything.

I am here, I told myself. I needed to be present. It was early in the morning, and there was only a young female student in the room, flicking through a glossy magazine.

The door opened and Dr Reynolds greeted me with a smile. "Hello, Emily. Come in."

I followed her into the consulting room, and by now the voices were chattering. This made me nervous.

"How are things?" Dr Reynolds asked me.

"My grandmother died last night," I blurted out. I looked away from her and heard the voices coming from the other side of the wall. I thought that they were trying to hear what I told the doctor. I fought to hold back my tears.

"I'm very sorry," Dr Reynolds was saying.

"I've only just found out. My mum telephoned me," I added.

Dr Reynolds was looking thoughtful, and then she said, "That's a real - well ... I was going to say coincidence, but that's not the right word. My father passed away last week. He had dementia like your grandmother, and had been ill for a while. So there are similarities in their illness at the end."

"I'm glad Granny's passed away, because she was suffering so much at the end," I said. "I went to visit her on Saturday, and she was very frightened. But I put on some old music, and she came round. She thanked me for what I'd done to help her."

Dr Reynolds smiled, and said, "Isn't that wonderful that you had a chance to say goodbye. You will have that precious memory to carry with you forever." She continued, saying, "With my dad we also sat around his bed, and talked to him when he was very unwell, and the process of dying had begun," she said. "I wanted to stay longer with him the last night, but there were things I had to do at home. Then he went, the next morning..."

I told her more. "I did these puppet shows with Granny until recently, which she loved. I've kept the fox and badger puppets."

"So a part of your grandmother lives on in the puppets." Dr Reynolds spoke in a kind tone.

I smiled, and then I felt tense again thinking that Granny had gone. So I said, "Do you think that people go anywhere when they die?"

"Well, let's hope they are joined by the people they have loved. So Dad will be with Marjorie," and she named other people whom I presumed were her deceased relatives. "If this is all there is, then it's a bit bleak and harsh, isn't it?"

The voices had gone, but I felt numb. *Daphne told me that I became 'psychotic' when there was something complex happening in my inner world. Surely, Granny's death could make me psychotic?*

"I'm worried about having a breakdown," I said.

"You won't," Dr Reynolds said. "It's normal to be sad. I felt okay after my dad died, as I'd kept busy with sorting out practical things. But then after a couple of days I suddenly found myself crying.

Afterwards, I felt better. So, if you find yourself crying, that's fine."

I really appreciated Dr Reynolds sharing her experience in this way, but I now began to feel anxious again. I said, "What happens if I hear more voices? I might even hear Granny's voice."

"It's quite common for people to hear voices after they've lost someone they were very close to," she said.

I didn't feel comforted hearing this. "Well, I'll take some pills, because I need to keep going with my PhD work."

"So what prescriptions would you like?" she asked me.

I started to tell her.

Later that morning I met a friend outside the Ashmolean museum; I'd first met her at the Mind peer support training course that I'd completed before I began my job. Mi-Cha was Korean, a housewife in her forties. She was easy-going and considerate. "I knew that you were very close to your grandmother," she said sympathetically.

"Yes," I said, as tears filled my eyes. "But she's been saying for a while that she wanted to go."

Mi-Cha said softly, "She was very old, wasn't she?"

"Ninety-four," I said.

"Still, it's a bit of a shock when it happens," Mi-Cha replied.

I nodded. "Shall we look round the museum?" I suggested.

"Yes, let's," she said, and smiled.

I stared at the blaring trumpets in the painting of Uccello's 'Hunt in the Forest', as I heard voices that seemed to project through the wall behind me. I was relieved to be in the museum with a friend. Still, a part of me was nervous, too. I moved across to another display-case.

I was glad to look at more paintings and statues, as I felt soothed by these. It was when we came to the little clay ram and clay horse that my sense of detachment was punctured. Granny would have loved these animals, and I now remembered the wind-up caterpillar and chicken that we used to have fun racing across the table in her nursing home. I suddenly felt very sad.

Perhaps Mi-Cha saw my unease, for she said, "Shall we get a cream tea? I've got a discount voucher."

"Yes, that would be great," I said, and managed a small smile.

Eighteen

In the days that followed, the voices were more intrusive and louder than usual. But only once did I hear what sounded like Granny's voice when I woke from a dream. "I'm not in pain now," she said in a faint, croaky voice. I took this to mean that Granny was pleased that she was released from her suffering.

I still felt at sea though. Daphne told me to focus on my job some of the time, as this would be a useful anchor at a very difficult time. It did help me to have a routine and work in the office during each day. I was doing my best to keep myself steady, when Mum called me one morning to tell me that the Oxford flat was going to be sold. The letting agent had contacted her to warn that they would have to serve an eviction notice, telling me to move out within two months. The flat felt like home to me, as I'd lived there for nearly four years. I couldn't imagine living anywhere else.

I felt really overwhelmed, and started to doubt that I could face Granny's funeral. But in my next therapy session, Daphne was adamant that I needed to go to it. "When you're in your fifties, it will matter to you that you've been to your grandmother's funeral," she said. These words stayed with me over the next few days, so I asked Marcus and Francesca if they would come to the funeral with me. I knew that if Marcus from Alcoholics Anonymous were there with me, I wouldn't drink alcohol at the lunch afterwards.

On the morning of the funeral, I felt really anxious. I was relieved when I heard a knock at the door. A smiling Marcus entered the flat, saying, "How are you feeling?"

"All right, but I'll be glad when it's over," I said.

"Well, it's a hard day for you, Emily," he said. "Right, put on some coffee."

"Is that dog hair?" he suddenly asked.

"What? Where?" I said anxiously.

"On your jumper," Marcus said, picking a strand of hair off my sleeve.

I looked down at my jumper and grinned. "I think it's one of Hannah's dogs."

"Use sellotape, that'll get it off," Marcus said.

There was another knock at the door. "That'll be Francesca," I said, and went to answer it.

"Those bloody buses," Francesca said, looking flustered. "I was waiting for one for twenty-five minutes. I was worried I wouldn't get here in time."

"D'you want some coffee?" I asked her.

"Yes, that would be lovely," Francesca said.

"Coffee's just coming up," said Marcus.

"D'you like the ribbons on my tights," asked Francesca, showing me her heel. Stitched onto her black tights were red and orange ribbons. "I thought it would cheer us up."

"I really appreciate both of you coming with me to the funeral," I said. Granny now came into my thoughts again. I felt a sharp pain inside me that I would never see her again. "D'you think I can bring the fox with me?" I pushed my hand inside the fox puppet that I'd used for the puppet shows I'd done for Granny.

"Yes, go on," said Francesca.

"Or is it childish?" I said. "Perhaps I'll just take him in my bag."

"Do whatever makes you feel happy," said Marcus. Suddenly I wanted Marcus to make me laugh by doing an impersonation. "Could you do a puppet show with the fox?" I asked him, throwing the fox in his direction.

Marcus pushed his hand into the sleeve of the fox puppet. Its head bent slightly, as he took a bow, then another bow, and Marcus said "Thank you, thank you", in an appreciative voice.

Francesca and I both laughed, and I felt less tense.

My mum, Aunt Janis and Uncle Jack had fallen out over the programme for the funeral over the past couple of weeks. But when we arrived in the reception room at the crematorium, members of the family were talking together, and a couple of people smiled at me. Tears pricked my eyes, but I was determined to hold my feelings inside me. My mum had already greeted me with a kiss outside, but now it was my aunt who came over. "It's nice to see you,

Emily," and she kissed me on the cheek. "These are my friends Marcus and Francesca," I said, and my aunt smiled and shook hands with them.

It suddenly felt claustrophobic and too warm in the room, and I was glad when we started to file through to the long room where the service would take place. I was glad to have Marcus and Francesca with me for support. There were more people there than I had expected. Smiling at me from the row in front was my cousin's baby girl, held by my cousin's husband. Several of my aunt's other grandchildren sat in the pews in front of me.

That was when the music started. It was uplifting, with slow melodic plucking, which sounded as if it was a harp being strung. I recognised it as Johann Pachelbel's 'Canon in D'. Then I saw the pall-bearers carrying in my grandmother's coffin. It was hard to think that it was her body inside there, lifeless and like white marble, when she had been so much more to me. Now I thought of the moment when the car had drawn into the crematorium's car park, and I had seen Granny's hearse. Close to tears, I had told Marcus and Francesca that Granny had once told me that "people were more important than things". This was when I had broken her expensive china when I was fifteen. She had been there for me when no one else had.

The music stopped, and the vicar started speaking. "Welcome to Vera's family and friends who have come together today to remember Vera..." I had worried that I would hear voices during the funeral service, but they were silent. Perhaps the most difficult part was when my mum went up to the front of the crematorium to read the poem, 'Do not stand at my grave and weep'. Mum had told me beforehand that she was determined to get through the poem without crying; Aunt Janis had bet her she couldn't, so my aunt had one of my cousins ready to take over the reading if necessary. All the way through that poem I stared fixedly in front of me, because I thought that I would be the only one crying, and I didn't want this to be the case. Another difficult part of the service was my uncle's address, as he kept talking about how Granny had been 'a difficult woman'. Was she? Yes, she was bossy at times, but difficult? I decided that the address that he gave was more about his relationship with Granny than it was about how she had actually been.

There is something quite obsessive about my coping skills when I'm faced with really difficult experiences. Granny's funeral was no different in this respect. So when it came to the last few moments before the orange curtain would close round the coffin, I said to myself in my head, *I'm going to make the most of the next decade. I'm going to do my interesting research, and visit America. I'm going to enjoy my life, like Granny enjoyed hers.* By then the orange curtain enveloped the coffin.

Playing now was Frank Sinatra's 'My Way', as it was known in the family that Granny had often got her own way. My aunt had wondered if it was cruel to play this piece of music, but my mum had insisted on the choice, as she thought that Granny was a 'bossy boots' and the song was an uplifting one on which to finish the service.

Everyone got up to file out of the room. I followed after them, sad, but relieved that the service was over. These were my emotions, and I wasn't feeling numb. Then I was shaking the vicar's hand, and stepping out into the sunlight.

Nearly a year has passed since Granny's funeral. My earlier fear of losing my equilibrium has at times returned, as I have faced some difficult experiences.

Shortly after Granny's death, I set up a support group for people who experience psychosis in Oxford. I had innovative ideas for getting along guest speakers to give presentations at the group on different aspects of living well with psychosis. But in the group I found it extremely difficult to share my own experience of hearing voices, and after six months I stepped down from my role as facilitator. I was pleased that a worker at Mind decided that she would continue to run the group.

In July my mum, who has bravely endured fifteen years of heart problems, and was seriously ill, had to have heart surgery. This meant that I was visiting my mum regularly in hospital, and feeling very stressed as I tried to support her.

During this difficult time, sometimes the voices would chatter, and on occasions I was afraid. Mostly the voices gave broken commentaries picking on things that had happened in the day; just a phrase here and there. Several times, when I was alone in the bathroom, I tried talking back to the neutral male voice for a minute or two, but it didn't want to have a conversation. Then in my head I would tell the voices to "Shut up and go away!"

I was very involved with my research, but sometimes thinking about trauma triggered my own troubling memories. I would stare at the wall, waiting for the voices to start again. Daphne had advised me to play music when the voices were difficult. So I listened to my favourite music, and told myself that the voices were just another noise. This way the voices didn't intrude too much, and I could keep working. I continued to see Dr Reynolds once a month; she listened to me and was supportive. I did still take psychiatric medication when I was distressed, as well as strong painkillers for my chronic back pain. I also kept up my weekly therapy appointments, and these made me feel more able to cope.

With my therapist I was able to reflect on the relationship that I had had with my grandmother, and I was encouraged to draw strength from the fact that I carry with me my memories of her. I have also been able to put boundaries on my relationship with my mum, so there is less conflict in our conversations on the phone, and now we meet once every few weeks to have lunch together. I'm fortunate to have kind friends, who are supportive when I'm going through difficult times.

I have become better at creating a work–life balance, where I give myself time for enjoying hobbies and having fun with my friends. My friend Beth has moved to Germany to live with her partner, and they have had a son. In August I visited Beth and her family in their cottage in a small village. Beth knows that I still sometimes hear voices when I'm distressed, and she doesn't stigmatise me for this fact. She understands that my childhood was difficult for me. I have an open invitation to stay with them whenever I'd like to. Before I left, Beth, of her own accord, mentioned the au pair job from all those years ago, as she remembered how distressed I'd been during that time. She said that she thought that Gloria was "a princess, and that's why she was a bitch" to me.

I continue to go to my research team's meetings, which I enjoy as I find them stimulating. I was pleased that recently I represented my research team at the 7th World Hearing Voices Congress in Spain, where I gave a presentation about my main findings from my interviews with voice-hearers.

Working has been one of the mainstays in my recovery. Fortunately, universities do make 'reasonable adjustments' for disabled employees and students. I now believe that many people who have mental health problems can work. Unfortunately, some psychiatrists and mental health workers continue to hold low expectations for recovery from psychosis, and this attitude needs to be challenged. For if people seek appropriate help and decide that they would like to work, then for many people this is possible. Daphne has suggested to me that the percentage of people with psychosis who are in work could be as high as 35-40 per cent.

I am still confronted with stigma at times. There continues to be considerable discrimination among the general public, who have had not had sufficient education about mental illness. The British Psychological Society's Report on 'Psychosis and Schizophrenia' (2014) showed that mental health service-users are only slightly more likely to commit violent crimes than those without psychiatric diagnoses. In fact, they are much more likely than others to be victims of violence. The newspapers fail to report these facts accurately, and when they do *report a story of mental illness, it is usually when someone has committed a terrible crime. You never read about the doctor or the civil servant who has psychosis alongside a successful career. I know through my research contacts that such people exist.*

I continue to enjoy my connection with music, with my weekly cello lessons and playing in the local orchestra. I find music to be very therapeutic, as it helps me to release my emotions. Sometimes when I wish to remember Granny, I play the Vera Lynn song 'We'll meet again'.

These days I appreciate the connections that I have with my work and with my friends. I hope in time to find a partner who understands me, and who I can have fun with. Over the recent years I have learned that I can feel fragile inside at times, but that I can still maintain my equilibrium.

Discussion Questions

1. Have you ever suffered from a mental health issue, or known someone who has? If so, what was this experience like?

2. What are the 'voices' that Emily refers to? How do you understand them? How does Emily's relationship to her voices change over the course of the book?

3. Why did Emily find it so upsetting to receive the diagnosis of 'schizo-affective disorder'? Could Emily have avoided seeing herself as a collection of symptoms?

4. Why does Emily turn to alcohol? What did alcohol offer her? In what way did Alcoholics Anonymous help her?

5. When Emily is isolated she starts to write poetry. How does writing poetry help her?

6. Why does Emily find it so hard to trust mental health professionals? Why are Emily's GP, Dr Reynolds, and her therapist, Daphne, able to build trust with her?

7. Emily is worried about losing her Benefits, which she "knew could happen if I was seen to be functioning well enough to work more than a few hours per week". What do you

think would have helped Emily to manage the transition to paid work?

8. Emily meets Rai, a trainer with lived experience, who hears over ten different voices at a training event. Emily is surprised to find out that Rai has just flown back from a conference in America. Why is Rai's example so helpful to Emily?

9. Emily stigmatised herself when she was on Benefits. She said that "I didn't usually go to community activities or social events, for fear that people would ask me, 'What do you do?'" How do you think Emily could have changed her attitude towards herself, so that she could have gone to activities or social events?

10. Describe Emily's relationship with her granny and her mum. How did their reactions to Emily's breakdown differ?

11. How did Emily's close friends Beth and Daniel help her in her recovery?

12. Emily is anxious about becoming a graduate student again. What support helped her to cope with the stresses and demands of her studies? Do you think that it is helpful for students with mental health issues to ask for 'reasonable accommodations' to accommodate their disabilities?

13. Emily did not meet her biological father until she was an adult. She describes this as 'long-term neglect'. Many psychologists and psychiatrists are now identifying an association between childhood adversity and abuse and psychosis (see Connor and Birchwood, 2012; McCarthy-Jones et al., 2015). Why do you think therapy helps Emily?

14. Emily enjoys her cello lessons, and playing the cello in a local amateur orchestra. How do these activities help her to build a social network?

15. When Emily is in Thessaloniki, Greece at the World Hearing Voices Congress, she wrote that "I felt lonely when I was surrounded by voice-hearers, because I knew that I didn't fully accept all the ideas of the Hearing Voices Movement. I wanted to stay in work, and I felt I needed to be discreet about voice-hearing and only disclose this to people I could trust." If you heard voices, would you tell your work colleagues? Who would you tell? Would you try to challenge stigma?

16. After reading this book, do you have a better understanding of what it is like to hear voices? Did it change your perception of 'psychosis'?

See: Connor, C. and Birchwood, M. (2012). Abuse and dysfunctional affiliations in childhood: an exploration of their impact on voice-hearers' appraisals of power and expressed emotion. *Psychosis: Psychological, Social and Integrative Approaches*, 4(1), 19-31.

See also: McCarthy-Jones, S., Romero, M., McCarthy-Jones, R., Dillon, S., Cooper-Rompato., C. Kieran., K., Kaufman, M., and Blackman, L. (2015). Hearing the unheard: an interdisciplinary, mixed methodology study of women's experiences of hearing voices (auditory verbal hallucinations). *Frontiers in Psychiatry*, 6, 1-16.

Discussion Questions for mental health professionals

Lionel Joyce OBE, CBE, Chair of the 'Road to Recovery Trust', Newcastle

Lionel was a Legal Services Commissioner, a Mental Health Act Commissioner, a member of the Public Guardian Board and CEO of Newcastle Mental Health and Community NHS Trust. He chaired the national association of NHS Trusts.

1. **Lionel:** Emily is an inpatient on a psychiatric ward for several weeks. Is this a therapeutic environment? Is this an environment in which people will be helped to get well, or simply contained, and prevented from doing things? The social worker / nurse interview is appalling, as there is no empathy to engage with the patient. This lack means there can be no positive development which could help the patient to get better. Let's reimagine this interview so it is supportive. Then, do a brief outline of how the interview could have been conducted so much more effectively, showing genuine empathy that leads to trust and progress.

2. **Lionel:** Emily has no referral to an Early Intervention in Psychosis team when she has a breakdown in her late twenties. The complete absence of care in the community is glaringly apparent. Both the need for structured activity that is supportive and enhancing is not

addressed, nor is the need for genuine emotional connection with other people who can emphasise the importance of building self-worth after such an episode. Let us now imagine what a genuine care in the community programme for Emily on her discharge might have looked like.

3. **Lionel:** Emily is allocated 12 sessions of cognitive-behavioural therapy. Is CBT the right treatment if it is 6 to 12 sessions? Is this anything like sufficient for a major mental illness? CBT, because it's formulaic, can often fail to deliver an empathic trusting relationship, as it clearly did in this case, leading to the patient being more frightened and resistant than when they started treatment.

4. **Lionel:** Was it a sensible course of action to treat a patient with a history of anorexia with olanzapine that leads to major weight gain?

5. **Lionel:** The referral to the community centre demonstrates firstly the lack of genuine relevant facilities for young people with intelligence and nous, and that in itself demonstrates the attitude underpinning care in the community, which is ghetto-ising, discriminatory and implies hopelessness. What would a programme have looked like that helped Emily to integrate into pre-existing community groups that could have included access to university / colleges and libraries?

6. **Lionel:** The staff in the day centre focus their discussions with Emily on her managing medication, or managing without medication, and there is completely inadequate support and advice to enable a proper strategy that would allow Emily to function at her maximum potential. What do you think would have helped?

7. **Lionel:** Emily's appointments with her GP in Oxford provide an example of really good clinical practice. Emily's GP offers time, achieves trust and empathy, and helps the patient by boosting self-esteem and responds positively to her needs. How can we help GPs to respond in this way?

8. **Lionel:** A trainer who is a voice-hearer runs the Camden Mind's Training for Facilitating Hearing Voices support groups in London. Rai is able to help Emily for the first time to have a different approach to her voices. This is the reason that the service-user's voice is so important in offering treatment and help, when she is part of and leading the therapeutic team. How could service-users be involved more in the design and delivery of training?

9. **Lionel:** Emily receives various mental health diagnoses, including 'schizo-affective disorder' and 'borderline personality disorder'. The harm done by using diagnosis as a label has been known for some time, and yet persists

widely through mental health services. How can we reduce the damage done by diagnostic labels? How can we pass on clinical information in a way that recognises the individuality of each patient, and of every patient's illness?

10. **Lionel:** Should patients have a choice in their community psychiatric nurse, so that they have a person with whom they build a relationship? Professionals talking to families about the patient without including them is a classic example of bad practice that should have been eradicated years ago: how can we prevent this in the future?

11. **Lionel:** Why does Emily turn to alcohol? How could mental health professionals respond to patients self-medicating with alcohol and drugs? Where does this become apparent? What would be an appropriate intervention?

12. **Lionel:** A nurse on the inpatient psychiatric ward recommends Alcoholics Anonymous. Would most clinical staff offer this voluntary sector support? Alcoholics Anonymous provides emotional and intellectual support to enable Emily to modify her behaviour in a way that is incredibly helpful to her illness. Can we roll this out, or does professional prejudice against 12-step recovery block this route?

13. **Lionel:** The police intervention is very impressive and effective. How do we support the police and continue to practise in this way?

14. **Lionel:** Emily's psychiatrist in her own time runs an open access group for her patients. This is fairly unique and is exemplary practice. Should it be offered by all community psychiatrists?

15. **Lionel:** Emily is stigmatising herself. This is compounding the problem of low self-esteem, fear and loneliness, and adding that this is all justified because Emily considers that she is 'mad and ill'. How as health professionals can we address this issue in treatment?

16. **Lionel:** Serendipity played an important role in Emily's opportunity to start a job, as this was suggested by her tutor who was a psychologist, who also knew about research opportunities and had not labelled or stigmatised a student for her illness, but saw it as an opportunity. How can we change attitudes to be more like this?

17. **Lionel:** Given the importance of work in preventing relapse, how should the government address the issue of the Benefits trap, and what response would be most helpful to a patient's recovery?

18. **Lionel:** Emily is included by her research team. Why is this an excellent example of inclusiveness of service-users?

19. **Lionel:** Emily has lessons from a cello teacher. What is the value of the arts, and or music, in supporting and enabling recovery?

20. **Lionel:** Emily's therapist challenges the way she views herself as being a service-user. Currently within the NHS, mental health diagnoses never stop being given even when a patient has been asymptomatic for ten years. The patient will still be considered to be suffering from 'bipolar' or 'schizophrenia' if they have once had this diagnosis. Does this need to change?

10158282R00109

Printed in Great Britain
by Amazon